MINI MAP+GUIDE

LONDON

T0286261

CONTENTS

EXPERIENCE

Left: An aerial view of London
Right: The skyscraping Shard in Southwark

NEED TO KNOW

KEY TO MAIN ICONS

🗺 Map		🚤 Riverboat	
🏠 Address/Location		⛴ Ferry	
☎ Telephone		🛈 Visitor information	
🚆 Train		🕐 Open	
Ⓤ Tube		🚫 Closed	
🚌 Bus		🌐 Website	

MIX
Paper from
responsible sources
FSC™ C018179
www.fsc.org

DK | Penguin Random House

Main Contributors Matt Norman,
Michael Leapman, Alice Park

Design Nidhi Mehra, Priyanka Thakur

Editorial Rachel Fox, Shikha Kulkarni,
Beverly Smart, Hollie Teague

Indexer Nayan Keshan

Picture Research Sumita Khatwani, Ellen Root

Cartography Suresh Kumar, Casper Morris

Jacket Designers Maxine Pedliham, Amy Cox

DTP Jason Little, Tanveer Zaidi

Delhi Team Head Malavika Talukder

Art Director Maxine Pedliham

Publishing Director Georgina Dee

Conceived by Priyanka Thakur
and Shikha Kulkarni

Printed and bound in China
Content previously published in DK Eyewitness
London (2019). This abridged edition first
published in 2020

Published in Great Britain by
Dorling Kindersley Limited
80 Strand, London WC2R 0RL

Published in the United States by DK Publishing,
1450 Broadway, Suite 801, New York, NY 10018

20 21 22 10 9 8 7 6 5 4 3 2

**The information in this DK Eyewitness
Travel Guide is checked regularly.**
Every effort has been made to ensure this book
is up-to-date at the time of going to press.
However, details such as addresses, opening
hours, prices and travel information, are liable to
change. The publishers cannot accept
responsibility for any consequences arising
from the use of this book, nor for any
material on third-party websites. If you
have any comments, please write to: DK
Eyewitness Travel Guides, Dorling Kindersley,
80 Strand, London WC2R 0RL, UK, or email:
travelguides@dk.com.

WELCOME TO
LONDON

Built on pomp and ceremony, London has become a cosmopolitan capital. This diverse city has it all: amazing art and ground-breaking music, royal palaces and historic pubs, futuristic skyscrapers and picturesque parks. Whatever your ideal break to London includes, this DK Eyewitness Mini Map and Guide is the perfect travel companion.

Steeped in history, from the imposing fortress of the Tower of London to graceful Buckingham Palace, it's easy to tread in the footsteps of kings and queens in London. The city is a cultural colossus, brimming with free museums and art galleries, from the National Gallery, with its Renaissance masterpieces, to the Tate Modern's cutting-edge performance works. London also boasts a vibrant music scene and the world's busiest theatre district, the West End. It's a paradise for foodies, where you can sample street food from around the world, as well as dine in an enticing array of Michelin-starred restaurants. Countless wonderful green spaces punctuate the city's heart, including eight royal parks, and swathes of bucolic bliss such as Hampstead Heath are never too far away.

London's charms extend beyond its centre to visitor-friendly enclaves all over the city. Head to the historic town of Greenwich, a UNESCO World Heritage Site and enjoy a stroll past the museums, cafés and markets and the magnificent Royal Park.

With so many different things to discover and experience, London can seem over-whelming. We've broken the city down into easily navigable chapters, highlighting each area's unmissable sights and unexpected delights. Add insider tips, a comprehensive fold-out map and a need-to-know section full of expert advice for before and during your trip, and you've got an indispensable guidebook to ensure that you see the very best the city has to offer. Enjoy the book, and enjoy London.

↓ The bustling streets of Piccadilly Circus

WHITEHALL AND WESTMINSTER

The seat of government for a millennium, Westminster is synonymous with two of the most stunning buildings in London: the Houses of Parliament and Westminster Abbey. The area is packed with a curious mixture of civil servants and sightseers, many of them making their way up and down Whitehall, the grand street linking Parliament Square and Trafalgar Square. You'll find few locals here, with its traditional pubs mostly the haunts of government workers.

↓ Inside the magnificent Westminster Abbey

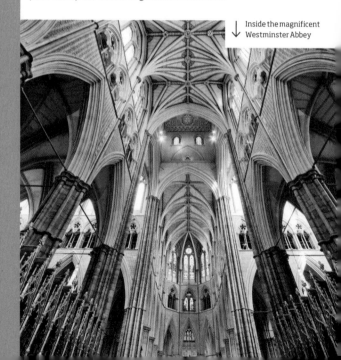

TURNER PRIZE

Every other year, Tate Britain exhibits the shortlisted works for the prestigious and often controversial Turner Prize, which was established in 1984. Representing all visual arts, four contemporary artists are shortlisted annually on the basis of their work during the preceding year, before a panel of judges picks the winner. Among the most sensational of the boundary-testing winners have been Damien Hirst's *Mother and Child, Divided* (1995) and the ceramics of Grayson Perry in 2003.

The stately façade of Tate Britain, home of British art

TATE BRITAIN

📍 I9 🏛 Millbank SW1 ⊖ Pimlico 🚆 Victoria, Vauxhall ⛴ Millbank Pier 🕐 10am–6pm daily (till 10pm last Fri, every month except Dec) 🚫 24–26 Dec 🌐 tate.org.uk

The nation's largest collection of British art, spanning the 16th to the 21st centuries, is held in a fabulous Neo-Classical building facing the river. The works include sculpture and modern installation pieces, plus a separate wing given over to the moody paintings of British artist J M W Turner.

The gallery exhibits a broad range of British art, from Tudor portraits and 18th-century landscapes to a large sculpture collection and modern art. Displays change frequently and the gallery's broad definition of British art stretches to work by non-British artists who spent time in the country, such as Canaletto and James Whistler.

The gallery opened in 1897, founded on the private collection of the sugar merchant Henry Tate and works from the older National Gallery. The Tate includes seven rooms added to display the paintings of J M W Turner, one of Britain's most revered artists.

The Turner Bequest, as it is known, was left to the nation by Turner on his death in 1851. It is displayed in its own wing, called the Clore Gallery, and consists of some 300 oil paintings, 300 sketch-books and about 20,000 watercolours and drawings. Major temporary exhibitions here always draw huge crowds.

WESTMINSTER ABBEY

📍 I7 🏠 Broad Sanctuary SW1 🚇 St James's Park, Westminster
🚆 Victoria, Waterloo 🕐 Check website for specific parts of the church
🌐 westminster-abbey.org

The final resting place of 17 of Britain's monarchs and numerous political and cultural icons, the glorious Gothic Westminster Abbey is the stunning setting for coronations, royal marriages and Christian worship.

Within the abbey walls are some of the best examples of medieval architecture in London and one of the most impressive collections of tombs and monuments in the world. Half national church, half national museum, the abbey is part of British national consciousness. Many of the leading lights from British history are buried or memorialized here, including poets and politicians, writers and scientists.

History of the Abbey

The first abbey church was established as early as the 10th century, by St Dunstan and a group of Benedictine monks. The present structure dates largely from the 13th century; the new French-influenced design was begun in 1245 at the behest of Henry III. It survived Henry VIII's 16th century onslaught on Britain's monastic buildings due to its unique role as the royal coronation church.

The West Front towers were designed by Nicholas Hawksmoor.

The imposing façade of the West Front with its two towers ↓

Inside the Abbey

The abbey's interior presents an exceptionally diverse array of architectural and sculptural styles, from the austere French Gothic of the nave, through the stunning complexity of Henry VII's Tudor chapel, to the riotous invention of the later 18th-century monuments. The latest addition is the 2018 Weston Tower, which provides access to the triforium and its Queen's Diamond Jubilee Galleries, packed with historical treasures.

> **INSIDER TIP**
> **Evensong**
>
> Attend the Evensong service to hear spell-binding choral music and get a glimpse inside the abbey – free of charge. The service also includes prayer and readings.

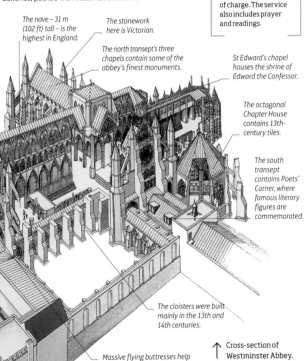

The nave – 31 m (102 ft) tall – is the highest in England.

The stonework here is Victorian.

The north transept's three chapels contain some of the abbey's finest monuments.

St Edward's chapel houses the shrine of Edward the Confessor.

The octagonal Chapter House contains 13th-century tiles.

The south transept contains Poets' Corner, where famous literary figures are commemorated.

The cloisters were built mainly in the 13th and 14th centuries.

Massive flying buttresses help spread the weight of the nave.

↑ Cross-section of Westminster Abbey, revealing the interior

HOUSES OF PARLIAMENT

📍 I7 🏠 London SW1 🚇 Westminster 🚌 Victoria ⛴ Westminster Pier
🕐 For details on visiting and to buy tickets, check website 📅 Recesses: mid-Feb, Easter, Whitsun, summer (late Jul–early Sep), conference (mid-Sep–mid-Oct), mid-Nov, Christmas 🌐 parliament.uk/visit

At the heart of political power in England is the Palace of Westminster. Built in Neo-Gothic style it lies beside the Thames near Westminster Bridge and makes an impressive sight, especially with the distinctive Elizabeth Tower.

For over 500 years the Palace of Westminster has been the seat of the two Houses of Parliament, called the Lords and the Commons. The Commons is made up of elected Members of Parliament (MPs) of different political parties; the party – or coalition of parties – with the most MPs forms the Government, and its leader becomes prime minister. MPs from other parties make up the Opposition. Commons debates are impartially chaired by an MP designated as Speaker. The Government formulates legislation which must be agreed to in both Houses before it becomes law.

The vast bell named Big Ben was hung in 1858 and chimes on the hour.

Government and Opposition parties face each other across the Commons Chamber.

↑ The green leather benches of the Commons Chamber, where the government sits

↑ The Gothic Revival masterpiece of the Palace of Westminster

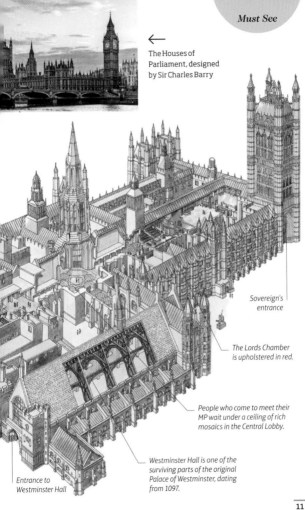

The Houses of
Parliament, designed
by Sir Charles Barry

*Sovereign's
entrance*

*The Lords Chamber
is upholstered in red.*

*People who come to meet their
MP wait under a ceiling of rich
mosaics in the Central Lobby.*

*Westminster Hall is one of the
surviving parts of the original
Palace of Westminster, dating
from 1097.*

*Entrance to
Westminster Hall*

Jewel Tower

📍 I7 🏛 Abingdon St
SW1 🚇 Westminster
🕐 Apr-Sep: 10am-6pm
daily; Oct: 10am-5pm
daily; Nov-Mar: 10am-
4pm Sat & Sun 🌐 english-
heritage.org.uk

This 14th-century building
and Westminster Hall
are the only remaining
vestiges of the old Palace
of Westminster, having
survived a fire in 1834.
The tower was built in
1365 as a stronghold for
Edward III's treasure and
today houses a fascinat-
ing exhibition called
"Parliament Past and
Present", which relates
the history of Parliament.
The display on the upper
floor is devoted to the
history of the tower itself.
The tower served as the
Weights and Measures
office from 1869 until
1938 and another small
display relates to that
era. Alongside are the
remains of the moat
and a medieval quay.

Big Ben

📍 I7 🏛 Bridge St
SW1 🚇 Westminster
🌐 parliament.uk/bigben

Big Ben is not the name of
the world-famous four-faced

clock in the 96-m (315-ft)
tower that rises above the
Houses of Parliament, but
of the resonant 13.7-tonne
bell inside the tower on
which the hour is struck. It
is thought to be named
after the First Commissioner
of Works Sir Benjamin Hall.
Cast at Whitechapel Bell
Foundry in 1858, it was the
second giant bell made for
the clock, the first having
become cracked during a
test ringing. The clock is
the largest in Britain, its
four dials 7 m (23 ft) in
diameter and the minute
hand 4.2 m (14 ft) long,
made in hollow copper for
lightness. The tower itself
was renamed the Elizabeth
Tower in 2012 in honour of
Queen Elizabeth II in her
Diamond Jubilee year.

A symbol the world over,
Big Ben has kept exact time
for the nation more or less

continuously since it was
first set in motion in May
1859. Now, however, it
stands silent, closed for
essential building works
until 2021 – tours are
suspended for the duration.

St Margaret's Church

📍 I7 🏛 Broad Sanctuary
SW1 🚇 Westminster
🕐 9:30am-3:30pm Mon-
Fri, 9:30am-1:30pm
Sat, 2:30-4:30pm Sun
🌐 westminster-abbey.
org/st-margarets-church

This late-15th-century
church has long been a
favoured venue for political
and society weddings, such
as Winston and Clementine
Churchill's. Although much
restored, the church retains
some Tudor features,
notably a stained-glass
window commemorating

← The Elizabeth Tower, seen
from Albert Embankment

THE CENOTAPH

On Remembrance Sunday every year, the Sunday nearest 11 November, ceremonies held around the UK honour those who have lost their lives serving in conflicts since World War I. The Cenotaph, a monument on Whitehall completed in 1920 by Sir Edwin Lutyens, is the focal point of London's remembrance service, when members of the royal family and other dignitaries place wreaths of red poppies at its base.

the marriage of King Henry VIII and his first wife, Catherine of Aragon.

Churchill War Rooms

📍I7 🏛 Clive Steps, King Charles St SW1 🚇 Westminster, St James's Park 🕐9:30am–6pm daily (last adm: 5pm) 📅24–26 Dec, 1 Jan 🌐iwm.org.uk

This intriguing slice of 20th-century history is a warren of rooms below the Treasury building, where the War Cabinet met during World War II, when German bombs were falling on London. The War Rooms include living quarters for key ministers and military leaders and the Cabinet Room, where strategic decisions were taken. They are laid out as they were when the war ended, with Churchill's desk, communications equipment and

maps for plotting military strategy. The Churchill Museum is a multimedia exhibit recording Churchill's life and career, and the display "Undercover: Life in Churchill's Bunker" features personal stories, objects and interviews with those who worked in the War Rooms. Booking ahead is recommended to avoid long queues.

↑ Telephones in the Map Room of the Churchill War Rooms

Parliament Square

📍I7 🏛SW1 🚇Westminster

Laid out in 1868 to provide a more open aspect for the new Houses of Parliament, the square today is hemmed in by heavy traffic. Statues of statesmen are dominated by Winston Churchill, glowering at the House of Commons. On the north side, Abraham Lincoln stands in front of the mock-Gothic Middlesex Guildhall. Millicent Fawcett – a campaigner for women's suffrage – is the only female represented in the square.

Downing Street

📍I6 🏛SW1 🚇Westminster 🔒To the public

Sir George Downing (1623–84) spent much of his youth in the American colonies. He was the second person to graduate from the nascent Harvard College, before returning to fight for the Parliamentarians in the English Civil War. In 1680, he bought land near Whitehall Palace and built a street of houses. Four of these survive, though they are much altered. King George II gave No 10 to Sir Robert Walpole in 1732. Since then it has been the official residence of the British prime minister.

Banqueting House

☑ I6 ☐ Whitehall SW1 ⊖ Embankment, Charing Cross, Westminster 🕙 10am-5pm daily (last adm: 4:15pm) ⊘ 24-26 Dec & 1 Jan 🌐 hrp.org.uk

This delightful building is of great architectural importance. It was the first built in central London to embody the Classical Palladian style that designer Inigo Jones brought back from his travels in Italy. Completed in 1622, its disciplined stone façade marked a startling change from the Elizabethans' fussy turrets and unrestrained external decoration.

Rubens's ceiling paintings, a complex allegory on the exaltation of James I, were commissioned by his son, Charles I, in 1630. This blatant glorification of royalty was despised by Oliver Cromwell and the Parliamentarians, who executed King Charles I on a scaffold just outside Banqueting House in 1649. Eleven years later, the English monarchy was restored with the coronation of Charles II.

The building is used today for official functions, and may close early when these are scheduled: check the website for details.

St John's Smith Square

☑ I8 ☐ Smith Sq SW1 ⊖ Westminster 🕙 For concerts only 🌐 sjss.org.uk

A masterpiece of English Baroque architecture, Thomas Archer's plump church looks as if it is trying to burst from the confines of the square. Today it has principally a concert hall, it has an accident-prone history: completed in 1728, it was burned down in 1742, struck by lightning in 1773 and destroyed by a World War II bomb in 1941.

There is a basement restaurant, open on weekdays for lunch and on concert evenings.

Guards Museum

☑ H7 ☐ Birdcage Walk SW1 ⊖ St James's Park 🕙 10am-4pm daily (last adm: 3:30pm) ⊘ Mid-Dec-end Jan & for ceremonies 🌐 theguardsmuseum. com

Entered from Birdcage Walk, this museum is under the parade ground of Wellington Barracks, headquarters of the five Foot Guards regiments. A must for military buffs, the museum illustrates battles in which the Guards have taken part, from the English Civil War (1642-8) to the present. Weapons and colourful uniforms are on display, as are some fascinating models.

Horse Guards Parade

☑ I6 ☐ Whitehall SW1 ⊖ Westminster, Charing Cross, Embankment

This is where the Trooping the Colour ceremony takes place each year, but you

← The Life Guards, part of the royal Household Cavalry

21st century. Visitors can see the working stables, and kids (big and small) can try on uniforms.

can see royal pageantry in action daily: Changing the Life Guard takes place at 11am (10am on Sunday), and there's a guard inspection at 4pm. This was Henry VIII's tiltyard (tournament ground); nearby is a trace of the "real tennis" court where the king is said to have played the precursor of modern lawn tennis. The elegant buildings, completed in 1755, were designed by William Kent.

On the opposite side, the ivy-covered Citadel is a bomb-proof structure built in 1940 beside the Admiralty. During World War II, it was used as a communications headquarters by the Navy.

Household Cavalry Museum

📍 I6 🏛 Horse Guards, Whitehall SW1 🚇 Charing Cross, Westminster, Embankment 🕐 Apr-Oct: 10am-6pm daily; Nov-Mar: 10am-5pm daily 🚫 Good Fri, 20 Jul, 24-26 Dec; occasionally for ceremonies 🌐 householdcavalry museum.co.uk

A collection of artifacts and interactive displays cover the history of the senior regiments based at Horse Guards, from their role in the 1815 Battle of Waterloo to their service in Afghanistan in the early

← Henry VIII's jousting grounds, now Horse Guards Parade

Westminster Cathedral

📍 H8 🏛 Victoria Street SW1 🚇 Victoria 🕐 7am-7pm Mon-Fri, 8am-7pm Sat & Sun; check website for service times 🌐 westminster cathedral.org.uk

One of London's rare Byzantine buildings, this cathedral was designed by John Francis Bentley for the Catholic diocese and completed in 1903. Its 87-m- (285-ft-) high red-brick bell tower, with horizontal stripes of white stone, has a superb viewing gallery at the top (there is a charge to take the lift). The rich interior decoration, with marble of varying colours and intricate mosaics, makes the domes above the nave seem incongruous. They were left bare because the project ran out of money. Eric Gill's dramatic reliefs of the 14 Stations of the Cross, created during World War I, adorn the piers of the nave. The organ is superb; there are often free recitals on Sundays at 4:45pm.

MAYFAIR AND ST JAMES'S

Home to some of London's wealthiest individuals (the word Mayfair screams "money"), neither of these elite areas are exclusively for the rich, with some good, affordable restaurants, cosy and welcoming pubs, and delightful gardens dotted around. South of ritzy, if traffic-clogged, Piccadilly, the streets of St James's are often surprisingly quiet, given this is the heart of London. There are historical buildings aplenty but, really, this is the place to shop for designer fashion and mingle with the moneyed.

Inside the decorative Fortnum & Mason's department store ↓

Must See

Works on display during the
annual Summer Exhibition

Did You Know?

The RA is also an
independent fine art
school – it was Britain's
first, founded
in 1769.

ROYAL ACADEMY OF ARTS

📍 H6 🏛 Burlington House, Piccadilly W1 🚇 Piccadilly Circus, Green Park
🕐 10am–6pm daily (till 10pm Fri) 📅 24–26 Dec 🌐 royalacademy.org.uk

Though it holds one of the nation's great art collections, the Royal Academy of Arts is most renowned for its blockbuster temporary exhibitions, as well as its popular annual Summer Exhibition.

A storied art institution that holds one of the country's most prestigious collections of British art, the Royal Academy of Arts (RA) celebrated its 250th anniversary in 2018. It has always been led by its elected and appointed Royal Academicians, artists themselves, whose works make up the bulk of the permanent collection and who help to deliver the Royal Academy Schools' programme. The collection is displayed across two Italianate buildings, palatial Burlington House and Burlington Gardens.

SEE THE SUMMER EXHIBITION

The highlight of the RA calendar and among the most talked-about events in British art is the Summer Exhibition, held annually since 1769. Anyone can submit their work, for a fee, to be considered for the show, making it a potentially career-changing event for unknown artists, though established artists exhibit too. Over a thousand entries are selected, ranging from film, painting, printmaking and sculpture to photography and architecture, and displayed for an admission fee.

↑ The exterior of the Royal Academy of Arts

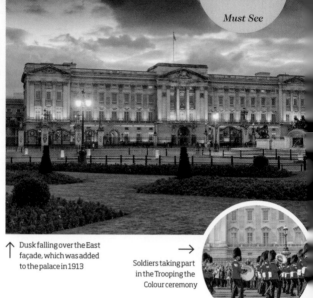

↑ Dusk falling over the East
façade, which was added
to the palace in 1913

→
Soldiers taking part
in the Trooping the
Colour ceremony

BUCKINGHAM PALACE

**♥ G7 ⌂ SW1 ⊖ St James's Park, Victoria ⊞ Victoria ⊙ State Rooms
and Garden: mid-Jul–Sep 9:30am–7pm (till 6pm in Sep); selected dates
Dec–May, check website 🆆 rct.uk**

**The Queen's official London residence is one of the capital's
best recognized landmarks. Visit its opulent state rooms
for a glimpse at how the royals live.**

Both administrative office and family
home, Buckingham Palace is the official
London residence of the British monarchy.
The palace is used for ceremonial
occasions for visiting heads of state as
well as the weekly meeting between the

Queen and Prime Minister. John Nash
converted the original Buckingham
House into a palace for George IV. Queen
Victoria was the first monarch to live at
the palace. She added a fourth wing to
incorporate more rooms.

EXPERIENCE MORE

Spencer House

📍H6 🏠27 St James's Pl
SW1 🚇Green Park
🕐Sep–Jul: 10am–5:30pm
Sun (last adm: 4:30pm)
🌐spencerhouse.co.uk

This Palladian palace, built in 1766 for the first Earl Spencer, an ancestor of the late Diana, Princess of Wales, has been completely restored to its 18th-century splendour (thanks to an £18 million renovation project). It contains some wonderful paintings and contemporary furniture. The house is open to the public on Sundays, for guided tours only.

Green Park

📍G6 🏠SW1 🚇Green Park, Hyde Park Corner
🌐royalparks.org.uk

Once part of Henry VIII's hunting grounds, this was, like St James's Park, adapted for public use by Charles II in the 1660s and is a natural, undulating landscape of grass and trees (with a fine spring show of daffodils). It was a favourite site for duels during the 18th century: in 1771 the poet

→

The royal St James's Park,
famed for its floral displays

Alfieri was wounded here by his mistress's husband, Viscount Ligonier, but then rushed back to the Haymarket Theatre in time to catch the last act of a play. Today the park is a popular place to take a breather from the city.

St James's Park

📍H6 🏠SW1 🚇St James's Park 🕐5am–midnight daily
🌐royalparks.org.uk

In summer, office workers sunbathe in between the flowerbeds of the capital's most ornamental park. In winter, the sunbathers are replaced with overcoated civil servants discussing affairs of state as they stroll by the lake, eyed by its resident ducks, geese and pelicans (which are fed at 2:30pm daily).

Originally a marsh, the park was drained by Henry VIII and incorporated into his hunting grounds. On his return from exile in France, Charles II had it remodelled in the more continental style as pedestrian pleasure gardens, with an aviary along its southern edge (hence Birdcage Walk, the name of the street that runs alongside the park, where the aviary once was).

It is a hugely popular place to escape the city's hustle and bustle, with an appealing view of Whitehall rooftops and Buckingham Palace, a restaurant open daily and an attractive lake.

Wellington Arch

⊙ F7 **⌂** Hyde Park Corner SW1 **⊖** Hyde Park Corner **⊙** Apr-Sep: 10am-6pm daily; Oct: 10am-5pm daily; Nov-Mar: 10am-4pm daily **⊠** 1 Jan, Good Fri, 24-26 & 31 Dec **⊛** english-heritage.org.uk

After nearly a century of debate about what to do with the patch of land in front of Apsley House, Wellington Arch, designed by Decimus Burton, was erected in 1828 (it was moved to its current position in the 1880s). The sculpture by Adrian Jones of Nike, winged goddess of Victory, was added in 1912. Before it was installed Jones seated three people for dinner in the body of one of the horses. Exhibitions are held in the inner rooms of the arch. A viewing platform beneath the sculpture has great views over the royal parks and the gardens of Buckingham Palace.

St James's Palace

⊙ H6 **⌂** Pall Mall SW1 **⊖** Green Park **⊡** To the public **⊛** royal.uk

Built by Henry VIII in the late 1530s on the site of a former leper hospital, this palace was a primary royal residence only briefly, mainly during the reign of Elizabeth I and in the late 17th and early 18th centuries. In 1952, Queen Elizabeth II made her first speech as monarch here, and foreign ambassadors are still officially accredited to the Court of St James's. Its northern gatehouse, seen from St James's Street, is one of London's great Tudor landmarks. The palace remains a royal residence for, among others, the Princess Royal and Princess Alexandra, and its State Apartments are used during official state visits.

St James's Square

⊙ H6 **⌂** SW1 **⊖** Green Park, Piccadilly Circus

London's squares, quadrangles of elegant homes surrounding gated gardens, are among the city's most attractive. St James's, one of London's earliest, was laid out in the 1670s and lined by exclusive houses for those whose business made it vital for them to live near St James's Palace. Many buildings date from the 18th and 19th centuries and have had many illustrious residents. During World

Did You Know?

Queen Elizabeth II was born at 17 Bruton Street in Mayfair, in 1926.

→

Stained glass at the Wren-designed St James's Church

EAT

Afternoon Tea at the Ritz

The poshest afternoon tea in town is accompanied by a pianist and harpist. Expect sandwiches, scones, cakes and tea. No trainers or jeans.

⊙ G6 **⌂** 150 Piccadilly W1 **⊛** theritz london.com

£ £ £

War II, generals Eisenhower and de Gaulle both had headquarters here.

Today, No 10 on the north side, Chatham House (1736), is home to the Royal Institute for International Affairs. In the northwest corner, at No 14, is the London Library (1896), a private lending library founded in 1841 by historian Thomas Carlyle and others. It offers guided tours at 6pm on some weekdays. The gardens in the middle contain an equestrian statue of William III, here since 1808.

St James's Church

📍 H6 🏠 197 Piccadilly W1 🚇 Piccadilly Circus ⏰ 8am–7pm daily 🌐 sjp.org.uk

Among the many churches Christopher Wren designed, this is said to be one of his favourites. It has been altered over the years and was half-wrecked by a bomb in 1940, but it maintains its essential features from 1684 – the tall, arched windows and a thin spire (a 1966 replica of the original). The ornate screen behind the altar is one of the finest works of the 17th-century master carver Grinling Gibbons. The artist and poet William Blake and Georgian prime minister Pitt the Elder were both baptized here. The church hosts concerts, talks and events, and houses a popular café. The outer courtyard hosts a food market on Monday and Tuesday, an antiques market on Tuesday and a crafts market from Wednesday to Saturday.

Handel & Hendrix in London

📍 G5 🏠 25 Brook St W1 🚇 Bond Street ⏰ 11am–6pm Mon–Sat 🌐 handelhendrix.org

A pair of Georgian houses on Brook Street have a couple of notable, very different, musical connections. The composer George Frideric Handel lived at No 25 from 1723 until his death in 1759, and his rooms have been restored to the early Georgian appearance they would have had during the composer's time, with portraits and musical instruments on display. The museum hosts changing exhibitions and regular recitals in an intimate performance space. In 1968, Jimi Hendrix moved into the attic apartment next door. These rooms were used for a time as offices by the museum, but have now also been lovingly restored to resemble Hendrix's former apartment, complete with 1960s decor.

Institute of Contemporary Arts

📍 I6 🏠 The Mall SW1 🚇 Piccadilly Circus, Charing Cross ⏰ Noon–11pm Thu & Sun; Fri & Sat noon–midnight; exhibition space: noon–9pm Tue–Sun 🚫 Public hols 🌐 ica.art

The Institute of Contemporary Arts (ICA) was established in 1947 to offer British artists some of the facilities available to artists at the Museum of Modern Art in New York. Originally on Dover Street, it has been situated in John Nash's Neo-Classical Carlton House Terrace (1833) since 1968. With its entrance on the Mall, this extensive warren contains exhibition spaces, a cinema, auditorium, bookshop, art gallery, bar and restaurant. It also hosts concerts, theatre and dance performances, and lectures. A modest fee applies to non-members, providing all-day access to most exhibitions and events.

SHOP

Fortnum & Mason

The finest foods, wrapped in teal, and sales floors are the hallmarks of Fortnum & Mason. Established in 1707, this is one of the city's most renowned and extravagant stores.

📍 H6 🏠 181 Piccadilly W1 🌐 fortnumand mason.com

SOHO AND TRAFALGAR SQUARE

Trafalgar Square can lay strong claim to being the epicentre of touristic London, a well-placed launching pad for much of what the city has to offer. Nearby is the liveliest part of the West End, with clumsily commercialized Leicester Square, lantern-strewn Chinatown and cool, unconventional Soho, the main LGBT+ district of London. Many of Soho's streets are replete with excellent independent restaurants, bars and theatres, making it the perfect spot for an evening out.

↓ The iconic Bar Italia in Soho

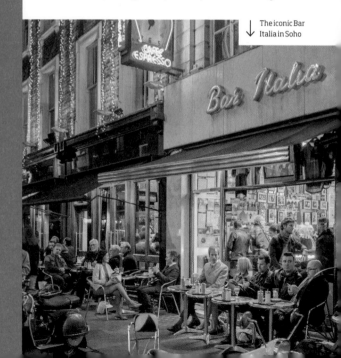

↑ The National Gallery, overlooking Trafalgar Square

GALLERY GUIDE

Most of the collection is housed on one floor divided into four wings. The paintings hang chronologically, with the earliest works (1250-1500) in the Sainsbury Wing. The West, North and East Wings cover 1500-1600, 1600-1700 and 1700-1930. Lesser paintings from all periods are on the lower floor.

NATIONAL GALLERY

📍 S3 🏠 Trafalgar Square WC2 ⊖ Charing Cross, Leicester Sq, Piccadilly Circus 🚆 Charing Cross ⏰ 10am-6pm daily (till 9pm Fri) 🚫 24-26 Dec, 1 Jan 🌐 nationalgallery.org.uk

Erected in the heart of the West End in order to be accessible by all, the National Gallery houses some of the most famous paintings in the world, by masters such as Rubens, Velázquez, Monet and Van Gogh.

Did You Know?

Close examination of the *Madonna of the Veil* showed it was a 19th-century fake, and not by Botticelli.

The National Gallery has flourished since its inception. In 1824 the House of Commons was persuaded to buy 38 major paintings, including works by Raphael and Rubens, and these became the start of a national collection. Today the gallery has more than 2,300 paintings produced in the Western European painting tradition. The main gallery building, designed in Greek Revival style by William Wilkins, was built between 1833 and 1838. It was later enlarged and the dome added in 1876. To its left is the Sainsbury Wing, financed by the grocery family and completed in 1991.

The National Gallery's paintings are mostly kept on permanent display. The collection spans late-medieval times to the early 20th century, covering Renaissance Italy and the French Impressionists. There are works by artists such as Botticelli, Leonardo, Monet and Goya, and highlights include Van Eyck's *Arnolfini Portrait*, Velázquez's *Rokeby Venus*, Raphael's *The Madonna of the Pinks* and Van Gogh's *Sunflowers*.

Examining the portraits of key figures in Britain's long and varied history ↑

NATIONAL PORTRAIT GALLERY

📍 S3 🏠 2 St Martin's Place WC2 🚇 Leicester Sq, Charing Cross 🚆 Charing Cross 🕐 10am–6pm daily (till 9pm Fri) 📅 24–26 Dec 🌐 npg.org.uk

Somewhat unfairly in the shadow of the National Gallery next door, the National Portrait Gallery, with over 210,000 separate works spanning six centuries, holds the world's greatest collection of portraits.

The gallery tells the story of Britain since the 16th century through the portraits of a wide cast of the nation's main characters, giving faces to the names familiar from history books. Founded in 1856, the gallery's first acquisition was one of the most famous depictions of William Shakespeare, known as the "Chandos portrait", after its former owner the Duke of Chandos. That portrait still hangs in the gallery today along with pictures of kings, queens, musicians, artists, thinkers, heroes and villains from every period since the time of Henry VII. Another of the gallery's oldest works is a Hans Holbein cartoon of Henry VIII, while there are Victorian portraits of key figures such as Charles Darwin, Charles Dickens and the Brontë Sisters.

 INSIDER TIP
Lunchtime Learning

A great way to dig a bit deeper into aspects of the collection, whether themes, backstories or the pictures themselves, is to attend one of the gallery's Lunchtime Lectures (£4). They take place on Thursdays, are delivered by staff or by visiting speakers and last approximately one hour. Buy tickets online or in person.

CHINATOWN

📍R2 🏠Gerrard St and around W1 🚇Leicester Sq,
Piccadilly Circus 🌐chinatown.co.uk

Though much smaller than its equivalents in New York City and San Francisco, London's Chinatown packs a punch. There are restaurants aplenty and a constant buzz that attracts countless locals and visitors.

Chinatown occupies the small network of pedestrianized streets north of Leicester Square and revolves around the main drag, Gerrard Street. Historically the Chinese community in London, who total more than 120,000, came predominantly from Hong Kong and were concentrated initially in Limehouse, in the East End. The current base in Soho was established in the 1960s, though the Chinese population is now widely dispersed across the city. Today, Chinatown is an intense little precinct marked by ornamental archways and, more often than not, strewn with paper lanterns. It is packed overwhelmingly with authentic restaurants and Chinese supermarkets, with bakeries and bubble tea shops, and herbal medicine, acupuncture and massage centres filling the gaps.

EAT

XU

Atmospheric Taiwanese restaurant which re-creates the look of a 1930s Taipei social club, with wood panelling, hand-painted murals and a tea room on the ground floor. The food is modern, a fusion of Taiwanese and Cantonese cuisine.

🏠30 Rupert St W1
🌐xulondon.com

£ £ £

←
Ornate Chinese arches stand over the area of Chinatown in Soho

EXPERIENCE MORE

Trafalgar Square

📍S3 🗺️WC2
🚇Charing Cross

London's main venue for rallies and outdoor public meetings was conceived by John Nash and was mostly constructed during the 1830s. The 52-m (169-ft) column commemorates Admiral Lord Nelson, Britain's most famous sea lord, who died heroically at the Battle of Trafalgar in 1805. It dates from 1842; 14 stonemasons held a dinner on its flat top before the statue of Nelson was finally installed. Edwin Landseer's four lions guard its base. The north side of the square is now taken up by the National Gallery, with Canada House on the west side and South Africa House on the east. Three plinths support statues of the great and the good; funds ran out before the fourth plinth, on the northwest corner, could be filled. It now hosts one of London's most idiosyncratic art displays, as artworks are commissioned specially for it, and change every year or so.

The Photographers' Gallery

📍Q1 🗺️16-18 Ramillies St W1 🚇Oxford Circus
🕐10am-6pm Mon-Sat; 11am-6pm Sun 🌐the photographersgallery. org.uk

This fore-running gallery exhibits work from both new and well-known photographers, as well as staging regular talks, workshops (especially for young photographers) and film screenings. Entry is free before noon, and when exhibitions are staged, the gallery stays open late (until 8pm) on Thursdays. There's a bar-café, and the bookshop also sells cameras and prints.

Piccadilly Circus

📍Q3 🗺️W1
🚇Piccadilly Circus

For years people have been drawn to gather beneath Piccadilly Circus's centre-piece, the statue of Eros, originally intended as an angel of mercy but renamed in the public imagination after the Greek god of love. Poised delicately with his bow, Eros has become almost a trademark of the capital. It was erected in 1892 as a memorial to the Earl of Shaftesbury, the Victorian philanthropist. Part of Nash's master plan for Regent Street, Piccadilly Circus has been considerably altered over the years and consists for the most part of shops selling souvenirs for visitors and high-street chains. It has London's gaudiest array of neon advertising signs, marking the entrance to the city's lively entertainment district with

← Looking across Trafalgar Square to St-Martin-in-the-Fields

its theatres, cinemas, pubs, nightclubs and restaurants.

Charing Cross Road

Q S2 **A** WC2
E Leicester Sq

Once London's favourite street with book lovers, with a clutch of shops able to supply just about any recent volume, many of Charing Cross Road's independent bookshops have been forced to shut due to rising rents. Several smaller, second-hand bookshops remain, however, including Quinto & Francis Edwards, which specializes in antiquarian books, and a handful in nearby Cecil Court. At the junction with New Oxford Street rises the 1960s Centre Point tower. This junction is one of the key sites for the huge Crossrail underground rail project, so expect traffic disruption

Leicester Square

Q R2 **A** WC2 **E** Leicester Sq, Piccadilly Circus

It is hard to imagine that this, the perpetually animated heart of the West End entertainment district, was once a fashionable place to live. Laid out in 1670 south of Leicester House, a long-gone royal residence, the square's occupants included the scientist Sir Isaac Newton

and the artists Joshua Reynolds and William Hogarth. In Victorian times, several popular music halls were established here, including the Empire (today the cinema on the same site perpetuates the name) and the Alhambra, replaced in 1937 by the Art Deco Odeon. The TKTS booth, sat in the square, is a must-visit for cut-price theatre tickets. There is also a statue of Charlie Chaplin, which was unveiled in 1981. The statue of William Shakespeare dates from 1874. Often crowded with visitors, the area around the Tube station here can be very congested at times; the streets of Soho and Chinatown to the north can be a better bet for a meal or drink.

St Martin-in-the-Fields

Q S3 **A** Trafalgar Sq WC2
E Charing Cross **O** 8:30am–6pm Mon–Fri, 9am–6pm Sat & Sun **W** stmartin-in-the-fields.org

There has been a church on this site since the 13th century. Famous people buried here include Charles II's mistress Nell Gwyn, and the painters William Hogarth and Joshua Reynolds. The present church was designed by James Gibbs and completed in 1726. In architectural terms it was one of the most influential ever

EAT

Café in the Crypt

Popular, licensed canteen with simple food under the arches of a church crypt.

Q S3 **A** St Martin-in-the-Fields, Trafalgar Sq WC2 **W** stmartin-in-the-fields.org

£ £ £

built; it was much copied in the US, where it became a model for the Colonial style of church architecture. An unusual feature of the interior is the royal box at gallery level to the left of the altar. From 1914 until 1927, the crypt was used as a shelter for homeless soldiers and others; during World War II it was an air-raid shelter. It is still today well-known for its work on behalf of the homeless and vulnerable. The crypt also contains a café, a gift shop and a brass rubbing centre, which is open daily. Lunchtime (free) and evening concerts (tickets required) are held in the church and weekly jazz evenings in the café. All are welcome at the daily services; check the website for times.

COVENT GARDEN
AND THE STRAND

The distinctive Covent Garden is always crowded, attracting visitors
and locals in equally large numbers. A dense mix of markets,
independent shops and restaurants sit side by side with fashion
chain stores and street performers looking for applause, and there's
usually a spirited family-friendly atmosphere. Running along its
southern border is the Strand, a busy road mostly worth visiting for
grand Somerset House, with its large and elegant courtyard – often
used for special events – cafés, restaurant and riverside views.

↓ A street performer
   in Covent Garden

COVENT GARDEN PIAZZA AND CENTRAL MARKET

📍 S2 🏠 Covent Garden WC2 🚇 Covent Garden, Leicester Sq
🚆 Charing Cross 🌐 coventgarden.london

One of London's most distinct and animated squares, Covent Garden comprises a bustling piazza filled with street performers and a market alive with shops, cafés and the occasional opera singer. It is a must-visit – a claim substantiated by the crowds who flock here.

The central, covered Apple Market, designed in 1833 for fruit and vegetable wholesalers, today houses an array of stalls and small shops selling designer clothes, books, arts and crafts, decorative items and antiques. The 17th-century architect Inigo Jones planned this area to be an elegant residential square, modelled on the piazza of Livorno in northern Italy, but the Victorian buildings on and around the piazza now, including the Royal Opera House, are almost entirely commercial. The market stalls continue south into the neighbouring Jubilee Hall, which was built in 1903. Despite the renovations, the tradition of street entertainers in the piazza has endured since at least the 17th century.

EAT

The Ivy Market Grill

The first of the the once-exclusive Ivy restaurant's offshoots. Smart Art Deco interior and a menu heavy on seafood and steaks.

🏠 1a Henrietta St WC2
🌐 theivymarket grill.com

£££

Strolling and snacking under the iron and glass roof of the Apple Market

↑ Courtyard of Somerset House with fountains and café tables

SOMERSET HOUSE

📍 T2 🏠 Strand WC2 ⊖ Temple, Charing Cross
🚆 Charing Cross 🚢 Embankment Pier ⏰ 8am–11pm daily 🖼 Courtauld Gallery: until 2020 🌐 Somerset House: somersethouse.org.uk; Courtauld Gallery: courtauld.ac.uk

This grand Georgian building, with four Neo-Classical wings around a huge stone courtyard, is an innovative arts and cultural centre offering a range of events and exhibitions in a marvellous riverside location.

Somerset House is best known as the home of the Courtauld Gallery, the city's premiere collection of Impressionist paintings. It is also a unique and popular venue for outdoor summer cinema and eclectic festivals, art fairs and installations. Built in the 1770s, its first resident was the Royal Academy of Arts. Later tenants included the Navy Board at the end of the 1780s. The building retains some striking architectural features, including the classical grandeur of the Seamen's Waiting Hall and the spectacular five-storey rotunda staircase called Nelson's Stair, both in the South Wing. Strolling through the wing from the courtyard leads to a riverside terrace featuring an open-air summer café and a restaurant, perfect for a sundowner. Below are the modern Embankment Galleries with a range of contemporary arts exhibitions, including photography, design and fashion.

EAT

Bryn Williams at Somerset House

Top-notch modern seasonal British cuisine with an emphasis on salads and grilled vegetables.

🏠 South Wing 🌐 bryn-somersethouse.co.uk

£ £ £

Fernandez & Wells

This light-filled café serves quality breakfasts and light lunch dishes, plus cakes, tea and coffee.

🏠 East Wing 🌐 fernandez andwells.com

£ £ £

EXPERIENCE MORE

St Paul's Church

📍 S2 🏛 Bedford St WC2
🚇 Covent Garden
🕐 8:30am-5pm Mon-
Fri, 9am-1pm Sun
🌐 actorschurch.org

St Paul's is the "Actors' Church" and plaques commemorate famed men and women of the theatre. Inigo Jones designed the altar at the west end to allow his grand portico to face east into Covent Garden Piazza. When clerics objected to this unorthodox placement, the altar was moved to its conventional position at the east end, but Jones went ahead with his original exterior design. Thus the church is entered from the west, and the east portico is a fake door.

The church grounds are a particularly pleasant place to pause – and surprisingly quiet in contrast to the hustle and bustle of neighbouring Covent Garden.

St Mary-le-Strand

📍 T2 🏛 Strand WC2
🚇 Temple 🕐 For services; check website for times
🌐 stmarylestrand.org

Now beached on a road island at the east end of the Strand, this pleasing church was consecrated in 1724. It was the first public building by James Gibbs, who also designed the church of St Martin-in-the-Fields on Trafalgar Square.

Gibbs was influenced by one of his early supporters, Sir Christopher Wren, but the exuberant external decorative detail here was inspired by the Baroque churches of Rome, where Gibbs studied. Its multi-arched tower is layered like a wedding cake, and culminates in a cupola and lantern. St Mary-le-Strand is now the official church of the Women's Royal Naval Service.

Royal Opera House

📍 T2 🏛 Bow St WC2
🚇 Covent Garden
🌐 roh.org.uk

Built in 1732, the first theatre on this site served as more of a playhouse, although many of Handel's operas and oratorios were premiered here. Like its neighbour, the Theatre Royal Drury Lane, the building proved prone to fire and burned down in 1808 and again in 1856. The present opera house was designed in 1858 by E M Barry. John Flaxman's portico frieze, depicting tragedy and comedy, survived from the previous building of 1809.

The Opera House has had both high and low points during its history. In 1892, the first British performance of Wagner's *Ring* cycle was conducted here by Gustav Mahler. Later, during World War I, the building was used as a storehouse by the government. Today, it is home to the Royal Opera and Royal Ballet companies – the best tickets can cost over £200 (though restricted-view tickets up in the "slips" can be had for as little as £12). Backstage tours are available.

Cleopatra's Needle

📍 T3 🏛 Embankment WC2 🚇 Embankment, Charing Cross

Erected in Heliopolis in about 1500 B C, this incongruous pink granite monument is much older than London itself. Its inscriptions celebrate the deeds of the pharaohs of ancient Egypt. It was presented to Britain by the then Viceroy of Egypt, Mohammed Ali, in 1819 and erected in 1878. It has a twin in New York's Central Park.

Museum of Freemasonry

T1 **Freemasons' Hall, 60 Great Queen St WC2** **Covent Garden** **10am–5pm Mon–Sat** **freemasonry.london. museum**

Looming over a corner on Great Queen Street, the Art Deco Freemasons' Hall was built in 1933 as a memorial to some 3,000 freemasons who died in active service in World War I. The headquarters of English freemasonry, the cultish traditions of this secretive organization are in evidence in the building's museum. Ceremonial objects are displayed around the main exhibit, a huge Grand Master's throne made for George I in 1791, topped with a crown and still used today. Peek into one of the lodge rooms where masons meet; it looks like a court-room, and is hung with portraits of previous Grand Secretaries (leaders of this Masonic lodge).

Neal Street and Neal's Yard

S1 **WC2** **Covent Garden**

In this attractive street, former warehouses dating from the 19th century can be identified by the hoisting mechanisms high on their exterior walls. Most build-ings have been converted into shops and restaurants. Off Neal Street is Neal's Yard, a bright and cheerful courtyard of independent restaurants and shops, most displaying vividly painted façades. Seek out Homeslice for a 20" pizza or try veggie delights at Wild Food Café; either will set you up for an afternoon of shopping. Neal's Yard Remedies offers potions and lotions, while Neal's Yard Dairy is one of London's best cheese shops.

London Transport Museum

T2 **The Piazza WC2** **Covent Garden** **10am–6pm daily (last adm: 5:15pm)** **ltmuseum.co.uk**

You don't have to be a train spotter to enjoy this museum. The intriguing collection is housed in the picturesque Victorian Flower Market and features public transport from t he past and present. The history of London's trans-port is in essence a social history of the capital, reflecting the city's growth and then promoting it. The museum houses a fine collection of 20th-century commercial art. London's bus and train companies have long been prolific patrons of contemporary artists, and copies of some of the finest posters on display can be bought at the museum shop. They include the innovative Art Deco designs of E McKnight Kauffer, as well as work by renowned artists of the 1930s, such as Graham

PICTURE PERFECT
Neal's Yard

A riot of rainbow-coloured walls, window frames and flower baskets, Neal's Yard, between Monmouth St, Neal St and Shorts Gardens, is the perfect subject to brighten any photo album.

Sutherland and Paul Nash. This museum is excellent for children (and they can enter free of charge). There are plenty of engagingly hands-on exhibits, including a London bus and an Underground train that children can climb aboard and pretend to drive. The museum also offers Hidden London, a programme of events and tours in disused stations across the city; check the website for more.

Savoy Hotel
📍 T2 🏠 Strand WC2
🚇 Charing Cross, Embankment
🌐 fairmont.com/savoy

Pioneer of en-suite bathrooms and electric lighting, the grand Savoy

←

The brightly painted former warehouses of Neal's Yard and the original branch of Neal's Yard Remedies

was built in 1889 on the site of the medieval Savoy Palace. A lavish £220 million refurbishment took place between 2008 and 2010, incorporating both the original Edwardian and the later Art Deco styles. The Gatsbyesque forecourt is the only street in Britain where traffic drives on the right. Attached to the hotel are the Savoy Theatre, built for the D'Oyly Carte opera and famed for performing the operas of Gilbert and Sullivan, and the Simpson's in the Strand English restaurant, where traditional roasts are served ceremonially from silver carving trolleys.

London Coliseum
📍 S3 🏠 St Martin's Lane WC2
🚇 Leicester Sq, Charing Cross
🕐 For guided tours; check website 🌐 eno.org

London's largest theatre and one of its most elaborate, this flamboyant building, topped with a large globe, was designed in 1904 by Frank Matcham and was equipped with London's first revolving stage. It was also the first theatre in Europe to have lifts. A former variety house, today it is the home of the English National Opera, and well worth visiting, if only for the Edwardian interior

with its gilded cherubs and heavy purple curtains. In 2003, the original glass roof was restored, providing dramatic views over Trafalgar Square.

London Film Museum
📍 T2 🏠 45 Wellington St WC2 🚇 Covent Garden
🕐 10am–6pm daily; last entry 1 hr before closing 🌐 londonfilmmuseum.com

Though previously an actual museum of film, this now misleadingly named place is really a James Bond museum, the Bond in Motion exhibition having effectively become the permanent and only display. The Bond memorabilia on show includes outfits and posters, but the exhibition revolves around an impressive collection of the original vehicles featured in the films. There are aircraft, boats, sleds and motorcycles, but it's the cars, many of them set against a moving backdrop from their respective movie, that usually attract the most excitement. Among the highlights are the unmistakable submersible white Lotus Esprit S1 from *The Spy Who Loved Me* and the quintessential Bond car, the Aston Martin DB5, first seen in 1964's *Goldfinger*.

HOLBORN AND THE INNS OF COURT

This is one of the calmest areas of central London. The traditional home of the legal profession, the relative absence of shops and restaurants means there are almost as many lawyers as visitors. The Inns of Court themselves are subdued havens of tranquillity, a maze of alleyways and gardens overlooked by city residents. Add to this the excellent small museums and the lovely Lincoln's Inn Fields, and you have a great place to escape the chaos and crowds.

↓ Stained-glass window, St Etheldreda's Church

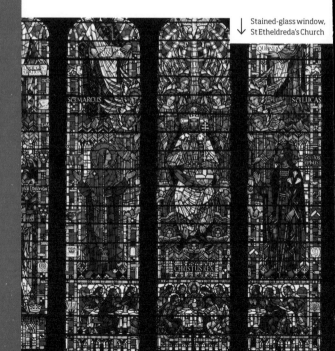

↑ A perfect place to relax, on the grass of Lincoln's Inn Fields

INNS OF COURT

Resembling the colleges of Oxford or Cambridge University, the four Inns of Court – Lincoln's Inn, Gray's Inn, Inner Temple and Middle Temple – are oases of calm in the middle of London and perfect sites for a relaxing and intriguing wander through history.

The Inns of Court are the centuries-old homes of the Bar in England and Wales, and every barrister must belong to one of the four Inns. Established in the late medieval period, barristers have long used the Inns for training and study and as accommodation. The leafy precincts, each with their own chapel, historic hall and landscaped gardens, make great places for a lunchtime picnic, and their jumble of passageways, hidden corners and courtyards are well worth exploring. Temple, the joint campus of Inner and Middle Temples, was first home to the Knights Templar, who were based here in the 13th century, and a rebuilt version of their church is a highlight of all four Inns. It is among the most historic churches in London.

> 💬 **INSIDER TIP**
> **Summer Spot**
>
> The best time to visit the Inns of Court are when the gardens are open: on weekdays between noon and 3pm. Middle Temple Gardens are only open in summer.

↑ Well tended, pretty gardens in front of Middle Temple

SIR JOHN SOANE'S MUSEUM

📍J4 🏠13 Lincoln's Inn Fields WC2 🚇Holborn 🕐10am–5pm Wed–Sun
🚫24–26 & 31 Dec, 1 Jan & a week in Jan for conservation 🌐soane.org

One of the most delightful and unusual museums in London, this extraordinary house, filled to bursting with an eclectic gathering of beautiful and peculiar objects, was left to the nation by the architect Sir John Soane in 1837.

Though laden with Classical statuary and other eye-catching and unusual artifacts, it is the interior design of the building itself that makes this place unlike any other museum. The house abounds with architectural surprises and illusions. Cunningly placed mirrors play tricks with light and space, and in the centre of the basement an atrium stretches up to the roof, the glass dome of which illuminates the galleries on every floor. In the picture gallery on the ground floor, walls turn out to be folding panels which knowledgeable curators open to reveal further paintings and, most unexpectedly, a floorless extension to the room itself, hung with yet more pictures.

↑ The museum, made up of three houses that Soane bought one by one

↑ Rooms filled with an eclectic array of ancient statuary

The Old Curiosity Shop provides a glimpse of London as it looked before 1666

EXPERIENCE MORE

The London Silver Vaults

📍K4 🏠53-64 Chancery Lane WC2 🚇Chancery Lane 🕐9am-5:30pm Mon-Fri, 9am-1pm Sat 🌐silvervaultslondon.com

These silver vaulzts began life as the 19th-century Chancery Lane Safe Deposit Company. Visitors are led downstairs, then through steel security doors to reach a nest of underground shops shining with antique and modern silverware. Prices range from modest to eye-watering.

Lincoln's Inn Fields

📍J4 🏠WC2 🚇Holborn 🕐Dawn-dusk daily

A former public execution site, many religious martyrs and those suspected of treachery to the Crown perished here under the Tudors and Stuarts. When the developer William Newton wanted to build on this site in the 1640s, students at Lincoln's Inn and other residents made him undertake that it would remain a public area forever. Thanks to this early protest, tennis is played on the public courts here year-round, while lawyers read their briefs in the fresh air.

The Old Curiosity Shop

📍J4 🏠13-14 Portsmouth St WC2 🚇Holborn 🌐the-old-curiosity-shop.com

Whether it inspired Charles Dickens's 19th-century novel of the same name or not, the Old Curiosity Shop is a genuine 16th-century building. With its wooden beams and overhanging first floor, it gives a rare impression of a London streetscape from before the Great Fire of 1666. The shop is still trading, currently as a handmade-shoe shop.

St Etheldreda's Church

📍K4 🏠14 Ely Place EC1 🚇Farringdon 🕐8am-5pm Mon-Sat, 8am-12:30pm Sun 🌐stetheldreda.com

Built in 1290, this rare survivor is the oldest Catholic church in England. First the town chapel of the Bishops of Ely, it passed through various hands over the centuries, including those of Sir Christopher Hatton, an Elizabethan courtier, who built Hatton House in the grounds and used the church crypt as a tavern. Rebuilt and restored several times, the church has some stunning stained glass.

Leather Lane Market

📍K4 🏠Leather Lane 🚇Farringdon, Chancery Lane 🕐10am-2pm Mon-Fri

Running parallel to Hatton Garden is Leather Lane Market. A traditional London market, it sells a bit of everything, including some tasty street food, and is a perfect place to pick up a treat or two.

Ye Olde Cheshire Cheese

📍 K4 🏠 145 Fleet St EC4 🚇 Blackfriars ⏰ 11am–11pm Mon–Fri, noon–11pm Sat

There has been an inn here for centuries and parts of this building date back to 1667, when rebuilding took place after the Great Fire of 1666. The diarist Samuel Pepys often drank here in the 17th century, but it was Dr Samuel Johnson's association with "the Cheese" that made it a place of pilgrimage for the 19th-century literati. Novelists Mark Twain and Charles Dickens were frequent visitors.

In recent years it has been argued that there is no real evidence that Johnson actually drank here; nevertheless, this is a great old pub, one of few to have kept the 18th-century arrangement of small rooms with fireplaces, tables and benches, rather than knocking through the walls to make larger bars.

Fleet Street

📍 K5 🏠 EC4 🚇 Temple, Blackfriars, St Paul's

England's first printing press was set up by William Caxton in the late 15th century. In around 1500, his assistant began his own business in Fleet Street, and the area grew to become the centre of London's publishing industry. Playwrights Shakespeare and Ben Jonson were patrons of the old Mitre Tavern, now No 37 Fleet Street. In 1702, England's first daily newspaper, *The Daily Courant*, was issued from Fleet Street – conveniently placed for the City and Westminster, which were the main sources of news. Later the street became synonymous with the Press. The grand Art Deco building with Egyptian-style detail at No 135 is the former headquarters of the *Daily Telegraph*. Next to the church of St-Dunstan-in-the-West (which largely dates from the 1830s) is a building adorned with the names of former newspapers.

The printing presses underneath the newspaper offices were abandoned in 1987, when new technology

Did You Know?

Sweeney Todd, the "Demon Barber of Fleet Street", is said to have had his parlour at 152 Fleet St.

made it easy to produce papers away from the centre of town in areas such as Wapping and the Docklands. Today the newspaper offices have also left Fleet Street, even though some of the journalists' traditional watering holes remain, such as Ye Olde Cheshire Cheese public house, and the legendary El Vino wine bar, found at the western end opposite Fetter Lane.

St Clement Danes

📍 J5 🏠 Strand WC2 🚇 Temple 🕐 9am-4pm Mon-Fri, 10am-3pm Sat, 9:30am-3pm Sun 📅 26 Dec-1 Jan, public hols 🌐 raf.mod.uk

Sitting proudly isolated on a traffic island, this wonderful church was designed by Christopher Wren in 1680. Its name derives from an earlier church built here by the descendants of Danish invaders, whom Alfred the Great had allowed to remain in London in the 9th century. From the 17th to the 19th centuries many people were buried here, and their memorial plaques are now in the crypt. Outside, to the east, is a statue (1910) of Dr Johnson, who often came to services here.

Nearly destroyed during World War II, the church was rebuilt and became the central church of the Royal Air Force (RAF). The interior is dominated by RAF symbols, memorials and monuments. Housed in elaborate glass cabinets along the aisles, remembrance books record the names of over 150,000 men and women who died while serving the RAF.

The church bells ring to various tunes, including that of the old nursery rhyme *Oranges and Lemons*, in whose lyrics the church features.

Dr Johnson's House

📍 K4 🏠 17 Gough Sq EC4 🚇 Blackfriars, Chancery Lane, Temple 🕐 May-Sep: 11am-5:30pm Mon-Sat; Oct-Apr: 11am-5pm Mon-Sat 📅 Public hols 🌐 drjohnsonshouse.org

The oft-quoted Dr Samuel Johnson was an 18th-century scholar famous for the many witty (and often contentious) remarks that his biographer, James Boswell, recorded and published. Johnson lived at 17 Gough Square from 1748 to 1759. He compiled the first definitive English dictionary (published in 1755) in the attic, where six scribes and assistants stood all day at high desks.

The house, built before 1700, retains some period features and is furnished with 18th-century pieces. There is a small collection of exhibits relating to Dr Johnson and the times in which he lived, including a tea set belonging to his friend Mrs Thrale and pictures of Johnson and his contemporaries. There are also replica Georgian costumes for children to try on. A statue of one of Johnson's favourite cats, Hodge, stands outside.

SHOP

Twinings

The oldest tea shop in London. Learn about the history of Britain's favourite drink, and try (and buy) a variety of brews from the world-famous brand.

📍 K5 🏠 216 Strand WC2 🌐 twinings.co.uk

BLOOMSBURY AND FITZROVIA

Though not exactly avant-garde, these relatively genteel districts have a pleasingly bohemian, laid-back air. Parts of Fitzrovia are densely packed with an enjoyable mix of restaurants, akin to Soho but turned down a few notches. Bloomsbury is the student quarter, home to several university institutions, a variety of independent bookshops and large garden squares. Its most famous location by far is the British Museum, but elsewhere Bloomsbury is characterized by a pleasing sense of studious calm.

↓ The Reading Room at the British Museum

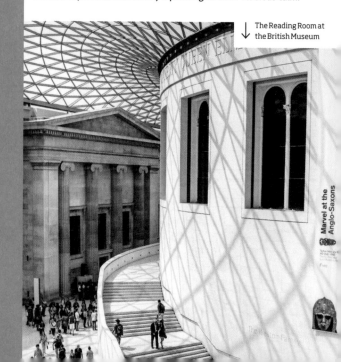

Marvel at the Anglo-Saxons

↑ Inside the Enlightenment gallery, formerly the library of King George III

BRITISH MUSEUM

📍 I4 🏛 Great Russell St WC1 🚇 Tottenham Court Road, Holborn, Russell Square 🚉 Euston 🕐 10am–5:30pm daily, till 8:30pm Fri 🌐 britishmuseum.org

The British Museum holds one of the world's greatest collections of historical and cultural artifacts. This immense hoard of treasure comprises over eight million objects spanning the history of mankind, from prehistoric times to today.

 INSIDER TIP
Eye Openers

The museum offers a set of free tours. There are daily "eye-opener tours" of individual rooms; and on Friday evenings the "spotlight tours" focus on specific exhibits such as the Rosetta Stone. Check the website for where and when to meet.

The oldest public museum in the world, the British Museum was established in 1753 to house the books, antiquities, and plant and animal specimens of the physician Sir Hans Sloane (1660–1753). The collection expanded rapidly and during the 19th century the museum acquired a mass of Classical and Middle Eastern antiquities, some of which still make up the top attractions here, such as the Rosetta Stone and the Parthenon sculptures. You can now see items drawn from a dizzying number of cultures and civilizations, from Stone Age Europe and Ancient Egypt to modern Japan and contemporary North America. There are sculptures and statues, mummies and murals, coins and medals, ceramics, gold and silver, prints, drawings and innumerable other man-made objects from every corner of the globe and every period of history.

↑ Russell Square, an oasis in the whirl of a busy traffic

EXPERIENCE MORE

Bloomsbury Square

📍I4 🏠WC1 🚇Holborn

This is the oldest of the Bloomsbury squares. It was laid out in 1661 by the 4th Earl of Southampton, who owned the land. None of the original buildings survive and the square's shaded garden is encircled by a busy one-way traffic system. (There is a car park below the square that, unusually for central London, nearly always has a free space or two.)

From this square, the entire Bloomsbury area was gradually developed. Noted for the brilliance of many of its inhabitants, it gave its name most famously to the avant-garde Bloomsbury Group. Look out for their individual plaques throughout the area.

St George's, Bloomsbury

📍I4 🏠Bloomsbury Way WC1 🚇Holborn, Tottenham Court Rd, Russell Sq 🕐Hours vary, check website 🌐stgeorges bloomsbury. org.uk

St George's was designed by Nicholas Hawksmoor, a pupil of Christopher Wren, and completed in 1730. It was built as a place of worship for the residents of fashionable Bloomsbury. In 1913, the funeral of Emily Davison, the suffragette killed by King George V's racehorse at the Epsom Derby, was held here. The crypt is the unlikely home of the Museum of Comedy, the first of its kind in the UK. Attached is a venue that hosts stand-up comedy performances in the evenings.

Russell Square

📍I3 🏠WC1 🚇Russell Sq

One of London's largest squares, Russell Square is a lively place, with a fountain, café and traffic roaring around its perimeter. The east side boasts perhaps the best of the Victorian grand hotels to survive in the capital. Designed by Charles Doll and opened in 1898, the former Russell Hotel – now the Kimpton Fitzroy – remains a wondrous confection of red terracotta, with colonnaded balconies and prancing cherubs beneath the main columns. The poet T S Eliot worked at the west corner of the square from 1925 until 1965, in what were the offices of publisher Faber & Faber.

Fitzroy Square

⊞ H3 ⌂ W1 ⊖ Warren St, Great Portland St

Designed by Robert Adam in 1794, the square's south and east sides survive in their original form, built in dignified Portland stone. Blue plaques record the homes of many artists, writers and statesmen: writers George Bernard Shaw and Virginia Woolf both lived at No 29 – although not at the same time. Shaw gave money to the artist Roger Fry to establish the Omega workshop at No 33 in 1913. Here young artists were paid a fixed wage to produce Post-Impressionist furniture, pottery, carpets and paintings for sale to the public.

Charles Dickens Museum

⊞ J3 ⌂ 48 Doughty St WC1 ⊖ Chancery Lane, Russell Sq ⊙ 10am-5pm Tue-Sun (last adm: 4pm) 🗓 1 Jan, 25 & 26 Dec, and occasionally Sat & Sun for events ⓦ dickens museum.com

The novelist Charles Dickens lived in this early-19th-century terraced house for three of his most productive years (from 1837 to 1839). *Oliver Twist* and *Nicholas Nickleby* were entirely written here, and the *Pickwick Papers* was finished. Although Dickens had a number of London homes throughout his lifetime, this is the only one to have survived.

In 1923, it was acquired by the Dickens Fellowship and it is now a well-conceived museum with some of the principal rooms laid out exactly as they were in Dickens's time. Others have been adapted to display a varied collection of articles associated with him.

The museum houses over 100,000 exhibits, including manuscripts, paintings and personal items, papers and pieces of furniture from his other homes, and first editions of many of his best-known works. As well as its permanent collection, the museum puts on special exhibitions and events, and runs a monthly "Housemaid's Tour". The garden café (no entry fee required) provides respite from the busy city centre and has a decent selection of drinks and treats.

SHOP

London Review Bookshop

A bookshop for those serious about books. The carefully chosen stock is testament to the highly respected literary credentials of its owners, the *London Review of Books* journal. There are knowledgeable staff members to help and chat, and a great little coffee shop too.

⊞ I4 ⌂ 14-16 Bury Pl WC1 ⓦ londonreview bookshop.co.uk

→

A bust of the great chronicler of London, at the Charles Dickens Museum

Pollock's Toy Museum

📍H4 🏠1 Scala St W1 (entrance on Whitfield St) 🚇Goode St, Warren St, Tottenham Court Rd 🕐10am-5pm Mon-Sat 📅Public hols 🌐pollock stoys.com

Named for Benjamin Pollock, a renowned maker of toy theatres in the late 19th and early 20th centuries, this is a child-sized museum created in two 18th- and 19th-century houses. The small rooms have been filled with a fascinating assortment of historic toys from all over the world. There are dolls, puppets, trains, cars, construction sets, a fine rocking horse and a splendid collection of mainly Victorian doll's houses. Parents beware – the exit leads you through a toyshop.

Wellcome Collection

📍H3 🏠183 Euston Rd NW1 🚇Euston, King's Cross, Warren St 🕐10am-6pm Tue-Sat (to 10pm Thu), 11am-6pm Sun, noon-6pm public hols 📅1 Jan, 24-26 Dec 🌐wellcomecollection.org

Sir Henry Wellcome (1853–1936) was a pharmacist, entrepreneur and collector. His passionate interest in medicine and its history, as well as archaeology and ethnography, led him to gather more than one million objects from around the world, now housed in this building. The museum's permanent exhibition, Medicine Man, includes more than 900 diverse objects, spanning from Napoleon's toothbrush to Florence Nightingale's moccasins. Changing displays cover a range of engaging topics exploring medicine, art and the human condition. Visitors can also discover the reimagined Reading Room – a hybrid area bridging library, exhibition and event space – relax in the café or enjoy afternoon tea in the restaurant. The Wellcome Library, which occupies the upper floors, is the world's largest collection of books devoted to the history of medicine

Grant Museum of Zoology

📍H3 🏠21 University St WC1 🚇Warren St, Euston Square, Russell Square 🕐1-5pm Mon-Sat 🌐ucl.ac.uk/culture/grant-museum-zoology

The heart of Bloomsbury's university district is Gower Street: on one side is the

The cheerful home of Pollock's Toy Museum

← Unusual exhibits at the Grant Museum of Zoology

Neo-Classical main building of University College London, designed by William Wilkins in 1826, and opposite is the original terracotta building of University College Hospital.

UCL owns several museum collections, including the Grant Museum of Zoology, established in 1828. It houses around 68,000 specimens – animal skeletons, taxidermy, mounted insects and other creatures preserved in jars (including one containing 18 preserved moles) – in crowded wooden cases, making it an atmospheric, occasionally gruesome, insight into the world of 19th-century science and collecting.

The Postal Museum

📍 J3 🏠 15–20 Phoenix Place WC1 🚇 Fatrringdon
🕐 10am–5pm daily
🌐 postalmuseum.org

Just over the road from the Mount Pleasant Royal Mail Sorting Office, once the largest sorting office in the world, the Postal Museum charts the 500 years of Britain's postal service in a series of engaging and interactive exhibits. The star attraction is Mail Rail, a 15-minute miniature train ride through tunnels that once formed part of the postal service's under-ground railway. The at-times pitch-black, narrow, atmospheric tunnels feature audiovisual displays along the way and deposit you in the original engineering depot. The museum itself contains exhibits spanning the full life of the oldest postal service in the world.

EAT & DRINK

Salt Yard

Excellent tapas combining Spanish and Italian cuisines.

📍 H4 🏠 54 Goode St W1 🌐 saltyard group.co.uk

Cosmoba

Classic Italian restaurant, serving pizza, pasta, meat and fish.

📍 I3 🏠 9 Cosmo Pl WC1
🌐 cosmoba.co.uk

££££

The Queen's Larder

Olde-worlde Bloomsbury pub with decent ales.

📍 I3 🏠 1 Queen Square WC1
🌐 queenslarder.co.uk

KING'S CROSS, CAMDEN AND ISLINGTON

Imaginatively converted from a downbeat industrial landscape into a collection of culinary, commercial and artsy hotspots, King's Cross has undergone staggering transformation in recent years. Not entirely finished, it's still gaining reputation – the same of which cannot be said of neighbouring Camden, where the alternative market and raucous venues keep the place thriving day and night. Adding yet more to the mix is well-heeled Islington, a more bourgeois district full of gastropubs.

↓ The interior of St Pancras station

EXPERIENCE

British Library

📍 I2 🏠 96 Euston Rd
NW1 🚇 King's Cross St
Pancras 🕐 9:30am-8pm
Mon-Thu, 9:30am-6pm
Fri, 9:30am-5pm Sat,
11am-5pm Sun 🌐 bl.uk

This modern building houses
the national collection of
books, manuscripts and
maps, as well as the British
Library Sound Archive.
Designed in red brick by
Sir Colin St John Wilson, it
opened in 1997 after nearly
20 years of construction.
A copy of nearly every
printed book in the UK
is held here – more than
14 million – and can be
consulted by those with a
Reader Pass (you can pre-
register for one online).
The real highlight, though,
is the Treasures Gallery,
which holds some extra-
ordinary items, such as
a Gutenberg Bible,
Shakespeare's First Folio
and lyrics by the Beatles.

There are other free
exhibitions, which change
regularly (these often
close earlier than the main
building during the week),
plus talks, discussions and
workshops. Occasionally,
the special exhibitions
have an entry charge.

Tours are highly
recommended; it's advisable
to book at least two weeks
in advance.

St Pancras International

📍 I2 🏠 Euston Rd NW1
🚇 King's Cross St Pancras
🌐 stpancras.com

St Pancras, London's
terminus for Eurostar rail
services to continental
Europe, is hard to miss,
thanks to the extravagant
frontage, in red-brick
gingerbread Gothic, of
the former Midland Grand
Hotel. Opened in 1874
it was one of the most
sumptuous hotels of its
time. Threatened with
demolition in the 1960s, it
was saved by a campaign
led by the poet John
Betjeman (there is a statue
of him on the upper level
of the station concourse).
The hotel has since been
magnificently restored and
has a swish cocktail bar.

Kings Place

📍 J1 🏠 90 York Way N1
🚇 King's Cross St Pancras
🎨 Galleries: 10am-6pm
Mon-Sat 🌐 kingsplace.
co.uk

This concert and arts venue
is perched on the edge of
the Battlebridge Basin and
Regent's Canal, a small
wharf whose moorings are
usually full of attractive
narrowboats. Performances
of classical, jazz, folk or
world music are regularly
staged, and there are two
commercial art galleries.
The open spaces are dotted
with sculpture and art.

EAT

The Lighterman

British pub-style food
in a first-floor dining
room with a spacious
terrace.

📍 I1 🏠 3 Granary
Sq N1 🌐 thelighter
man.co.uk

££££

Rotunda

Enjoy the plant-filled
terrace on the canal,
perfect on a sunny day.

📍 J1 🏠 Kings Pl, 90
York Way N1
🌐 rotundabar
andrestaurant.co.uk

££££

German Gymnasium

Hearty German food in
a modern continental
grand café.

📍 I1 🏠 1 King's
Blvd N1
🌐 german
gymnasium.com

££££

Estorick Collection of Modern Italian Art

♀ L1 🏛 39a Canonbury Sq N1 ⊖ Highbury & Islington 🕐 11am-6pm Wed-Sat, noon-5pm Sun 🌐 estorickcollection.com

Based on American and Anglo-German couple Eric and Salome Estorick's collection of modern Italian art, this is one of the more surprising of Islington's assets. It is housed in an unpretentious Georgian building with a delightful garden, partly occupied by an inviting café. At the core of the collection are important works of the Italian Futurism movement: paintings and drawings by the likes of Umberto Boccioni, Carlo Carrà, Luigi Russolo and Gino Severini. Spread over six galleries on three floors, there is plenty of striking modern Italian art of other genres, including sculpture.

The Jewish Museum

♀ G1 🏛 129-131 Albert St NW1 ⊖ Camden Town 🕐 10am-5pm Sat-Thu, 10am-2pm Fri 🚫 Jewish hols, 25 & 26 Dec, 1 Jan 🌐 jewishmuseum.org.uk

London's Jewish Museum was founded in 1932 in Bloomsbury, and it has occupied several locations – at one point it was split between two sites, in Finchley and Camden. In 2007 the museum celebrated its 75th anniversary by starting work to bring the two collections together in a single building.

Reopened in 2010, the museum today has large galleries, education facilities and displays for children. Celebrating Jewish life in Britain from the Middle Ages onwards, the museum is packed with memorabilia. It has important collections of Jewish ceremonial objects and some illuminated marriage contracts. The highlight is a 17th- or 18th-century Venetian synagogue ark. There is also an exhibition on the Holocaust.

The Angel, Islington and Upper Street

♀ K1 🏛 Islington N1 ⊖ Angel, Highbury & Islington

One of the destination high streets in north London, Upper Street runs for 1.5 km (1 mile) between Angel and Highbury & Islington tube stations. Lively day and night, the street is one long parade of restaurants, cafés, pubs, bars, fashion boutiques and a contrasting mix of civic buildings, churches, an arthouse cinema and a live music

and clubbing venue. Parallel to the main drag is Camden Passage, an alleyway even more densely packed with shops, cafés and covered markets. It's a popular place for antiques hunters looking for the latest bargain.

The area to the south of the high street known as Angel takes its name from a 17th-century coaching inn on the corner of Pentonville Road, since replaced by the current sand-coloured structure, crowned with an elegant domed cupola. Built in 1903 as the Angel Hotel it now houses a bank and offices.

Granary Square

♀ I1 ⊖ King's Cross St Pancras 🌐 kingscross. co.uk

Urban regeneration has transformed this area

↑ Bright lights of Granary Square, King's Cross

behind King's Cross station into a cultural and social hub, with major building projects still ongoing. The focus of the area is attractive Granary Square, which leads down to Regent's Canal. It is dominated by magnificent fountains that dance to an ever-changing pattern of lights, a magnet for small children on hot days. There are also a number of good restaurants and bars, and a popular food market.

Occupying the former King's Cross Goods Yards offices, built in 1850, is the House of Illustration. These three small rooms form the UK's only gallery dedicated to illustration.

Founded by Sir Quentin Blake, best known for his illustrations of Roald Dahl's children's books, the gallery stages an eclectic programme of exhibitions, past examples featuring work from Soviet Russia, Japan, Thailand and North Korea. Displays cover a broad range of techniques and mediums, including graphic design, animation, scientific drawings, picture books and political cartoons.

Camden Market
9 G1 **Ⓜ** NW1
Ⓔ Camden Town, Chalk Farm **🕙** 10am–6pm daily; some cafés and bars open later
w camdenmarket.com

The huge Camden Market is really a series of interconnected markets running along Chalk Farm Road and Camden High Street. Packed at the weekends, most of the shops and some of the stalls are also open on weekdays. The first market here was a small crafts market set up at Camden Lock in 1975, and today the lock, crossing the Regent's Canal, is the focus of this sprawling agglomeration.

Independently trading on an industrial scale, the warren of hundreds of stalls, units and shops occupy a network of restored and converted Victorian warehouses.

The market has been at the forefront of alternative fashion since the days of punk, and the current jumble of hand-made and vintage clothes and jewellery, arts and crafts, records and music memorabilia, and all kinds of quirky one-offs maintain the market's place among the most original shopping destinations in the city. This is also street food heaven, with scores of stalls, cafés and wonderfully inelegant restaurants dishing out authentic nosh from all over the world.

Some of the more interesting stalls are in the Stables Market towards the Chalk Farm end, where you will also find a statue of Camden habituée, the late singer-songwriter Amy Winehouse.

THE CITY

The towering skyscrapers of the City make up London's traditional financial district, where corporates in suits scurry around during the week, making it a bustling place at lunchtimes but an eerily deserted one during the weekend. Also the historical heart of the city, with traces of the Roman occupation in places, the sights are dispersed over a relatively wide area, but there are plenty of them, including London's highest concentration of medieval and early modern churches, crowned by the most famous church of all, St Paul's Cathedral.

The iconic St Paul's Cathedral in the middle of the City

The imposing walls of the historic Tower of London ↑

TOWER OF LONDON

📍05 🏰 Tower Hill EC3 ⊖ Tower Hill, DLR Tower Gateway 🚆 Fenchurch Street
🕐 9am–5:30pm Tue–Sat; 10am–5:30pm Sun & Mon (till 4:30pm Nov–Feb) 🌐 hrp.org.uk

A former fortress, palace and prison, the Tower of London attracts nearly three million visitors a year, who come to see the Crown Jewels and to hear tales of its dark and intriguing history.

↑ Yeoman Warders guarding the Tower

For much of its 900-year history, the Tower was somewhere to be feared. Those who had committed treason or threatened the throne were held within its dank walls – many did not get out alive, and some were tortured before meeting violent deaths on nearby Tower Hill.

The Tower has been a tourist attraction since the reign of Charles II (1660–85), when both the Crown Jewels and the collection of armour were first shown to the public, and it remains popular today. Come to discover the brutality of royal regimes, the curious menagerie that once called the Tower home and the regalia of Britain's kings and queens.

ST PAUL'S CATHEDRAL

📍 L5 🏛 Ludgate Hill EC4 🚇 St Paul's, Mansion House 🚉 City Thameslink, Blackfriars 🕐 Cathedral: 8:30am–4:30pm (last adm: 4pm) Mon–Sat; Galleries: 9:30am–4:15pm Mon–Sat 🌐 stpauls.co.uk

Holding its own against the towering skyscrapers of the City, the enormous dome of St Paul's Cathedral stands out as the star of the area's churches. Completed in 1711, Sir Christopher Wren's Baroque masterpiece was England's first purpose-built Protestant cathedral, and has many similarities with St Peter's in Rome, notably in its ornate dome.

Following the Great Fire of London in 1666, the medieval cathedral of St Paul's was left in ruins. The authorities turned to Christopher Wren to rebuild it, but his ideas met with considerable resistance from the conservative Dean and Chapter. Wren's 1672 Great Model plan was rejected and a watered-down plan was finally agreed in 1675. Wren's determination paid off, though: the cathedral is considered his greatest masterpiece. Its dome is one of

the largest in the world, standing 111 m (365 ft) high and weighing 65,000 tonnes.

The cathedral has a strong choral tradition and is famed for its music, with regular concerts and organ recitals.

CHRISTOPHER WREN

Sir Christopher Wren (1632–1723) played an integral part in the restoration of London after the Great Fire of 1666. He devised a new city plan, replacing the narrow streets with wide avenues radiating from piazzas. His plan was rejected, but he was commissioned to build 52 new churches; 31 have survived various threats of demolition and the bombs of World War II, although six have only partial remains. Wren's great masterpiece is the massive St Paul's, while nearly as splendid is St Stephen Walbrook, his domed church of 1672–7. Other landmarks are St Bride's, off Fleet Street, said to have inspired the traditional shape of wedding cakes, and St Mary-le-Bow in Cheapside.

↑ The Whispering Gallery allows views down to the wide expanse of the crossing, the area under the dome.

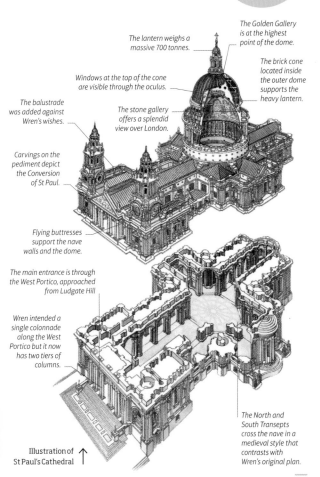

The Golden Gallery is at the highest point of the dome.

The lantern weighs a massive 700 tonnes.

The brick cone located inside the outer dome supports the heavy lantern.

Windows at the top of the cone are visible through the oculus.

The balustrade was added against Wren's wishes.

The stone gallery offers a splendid view over London.

Carvings on the pediment depict the Conversion of St Paul.

Flying buttresses support the nave walls and the dome.

The main entrance is through the West Portico, approached from Ludgate Hill

Wren intended a single colonnade along the West Portico but it now has two tiers of columns.

The North and South Transepts cross the nave in a medieval style that contrasts with Wren's original plan.

Illustration of St Paul's Cathedral

EXPERIENCE MORE

Bank of England Museum

📍 M5 🏛 Bartholomew Lane EC2 🚇 Bank ⏰ 10am–5pm Mon–Fri 🚫 Public hols 🌐 bankofengland.co.uk

The Bank of England was set up in 1694 to raise money for foreign wars. It grew to become Britain's central bank, and also issues currency notes. Sir John Soane was the architect of the 1788 bank building on this site, but only the exterior wall of his design has survived. The rest was destroyed in the 1920s and 1930s when, the building was enlarged by Sir Herbert Baker. The only part of Soane's design left today is the curtain wall around the outside of the building. There is now a reconstruction of Soane's stock office of 1793 in the museum. As well as images illustrating the architectural history of the building, the museum reveals the work of the Bank and financial system, and there is an interactive exhibit where visitors can set monetary policy. Glittering gold bars (which you can touch), silver-plated decorations and a Roman mosaic floor, which was discovered during the rebuilding, are among the items on display, along with a unique collection of banknotes.

The Royal Exchange

📍 N5 🏛 EC3 🚇 Bank 🌐 theroyalexchange. co.uk

Sir Thomas Gresham, an Elizabethan merchant and courtier, founded the Royal Exchange in 1565 as a centre for commerce of all kinds. The original building was centred on a vast courtyard where merchants and tradesmen did business. Queen Elizabeth I gave it its royal title and it is still one of the sites from which a new monarch is announced. Dating from 1844, this is the third splendid building on the site since Gresham's. The building is now a luxurious shopping centre with designer stores and a branch of Fortnum and Mason with an elegant bar and café.

St Stephen Walbrook

📍 M5 🏛 39 Walbrook EC4 🚇 Bank, Cannon St ⏰ 10am–4pm Mon, Tue & Thu, 11am–3pm Wed, 10am–3:30pm Fri 🌐 ststephenwalbrook.net

The Lord Mayor's parish church was built by architect Christopher Wren in 1672–9 and it is considered the finest of his City churches. The deep, coffered dome, with its ornate plasterwork, was a forerunner of St Paul's Cathedral.

St Stephen's airy columned interior comes as a surprise after its plain exterior. The font cover and pulpit canopy are decorated with exquisite carved figures that contrast strongly with the stark simplicity of Henry

→

The Neo-Classical façade of the Royal Exchange

Moore's massive white stone altar (1972), installed in 1987.

However, perhaps the most moving monument of all is a telephone in a glass box. This is a tribute to Rector Chad Varah who, in 1953, founded the Samaritans, a volunteer-staffed telephone helpline for people in emotional need.

The church is also the home of the London Internet Church, which brings together people from all over the world to worship and discuss Christianity. There are free lunchtime music recitals on Tuesdays (1pm) and Fridays (12:30pm), to which you are welcome to bring and eat a packed lunch.

Monument
📍 N5 🏛 Monument St EC3 🚇 Monument ⏰ Platform: 9:30am-5:30pm daily (to 6pm Apr-Sep) 🚫 24-26 Dec 🌐 themonument.info

The column designed by Wren to commemorate the Great Fire of London of 1666 is the tallest isolated stone column in the world. It is 61.5 m (202 ft) high and is said to be 61.5 m west of where the fire started, in Pudding Lane. Reliefs around the column's base show Charles II restoring the city. It's a tough climb up 311 steps to the top of the column, but the views from the viewing platform are spectacular.

Museum of London
📍 L4 🏛 150 London Wall EC2 🚇 Barbican, St Paul's, Moorgate ⏰ 10am-6pm daily 🌐 museumof london.org.uk

Opened in 1976 on the edge of the Barbican Estate, this museum provides a lively account of London life from prehistoric times to the present day. The eclectic set of displays, which are laid out chronologically, range from detailed models and life-sized sets to items recovered from archaeological digs, photographs and recordings of Londoners talking about their lives.

Prehistory exhibits, such as flint hand axes found in the gravels under the modern city, begin on the entrance level and visitors can walk through Roman and medieval London galleries to the War, Plague and Fire exhibit, which includes a display on the Great Fire of 1666.

On the lowest level, the history of London after the disastrous fire up to the present day is explored. The Lord Mayor of London's spectacular State Coach is on show here. Finely carved and painted, this gilded coach from c 1757 is paraded once a year during the Lord Mayor's Show. The Victorian Walk uses several original shopfronts to re-create the atmosphere of late-19th-century London. There are

EAT

José Pizarro
Classic Spanish tapas and inventive dishes.

📍 N4 🏛 36 Broadgate Circle EC2 🌐 jose pizarro.com

£ £ £

The Jugged Hare
Gastropub serving excellent game dishes.

📍 M3 🏛 49 Chiswell St EC1 🌐 thejugged hare.com

£ £ £

also the bronze and cast-iron Brandt Edgar lifts from Selfridges department store on Oxford Street and unusual items such as a 1964 Beatles dress printed with the faces of the Fab Four.

One of the newest permanent galleries is the London 2012 Cauldron, the centrepiece of the opening and closing ceremonies at the London Olympics. Photographs, videos, diagrams and the copper petal elements which rose together to form the Olympic Flame combine to describe the spectacle and the ingenuity of the design.

←

Tower Bridge, an enduring symbol of London, at sunset

Leadenhall Market

📍 N5 🏛 Gracechurch St EC3 🚇 Bank, Monument ⏰ Times vary; check website 🌐 leadenhall market.co.uk

There has been a food market here, on the site of a Roman forum, since the Middle Ages.

Today's ornate Victorian covered shopping arcade was designed in 1881 by Sir Horace Jones. Leadenhall is now home to boutique wine shops, cheesemongers, florists and fine food shops, along with several traditional pubs and wine bars. At Christmas the decorated stores are an attractive sight.

Tower Bridge

📍 O6 🏛 SE1 🚇 Tower Hill ⏰ Exhibition: Apr-Sep: 10am-5:30pm daily; Oct-Mar: 9:30am-5pm daily 🚫 24-26 Dec 🌐 towerbridge.org.uk

Completed in 1894, this flamboyant piece of Victorian engineering is a symbol of London. Its pinnacled towers and linking catwalk support the mechanism for raising the roadway when big ships have to pass through, or for special occasions; check the website for details. When raised, the bridge is 40 m (135 ft) high.

Walking across the bridge is free but access to the elevated walkways requires a ticket. This includes entry to the exhibition in the North Tower and the Engine Rooms, reached via the South Tower, a look at the steam engine that powered the lifting machinery until 1976, when the system was electrified.

St Bartholomew-the-Great

📍 L4 🏛 West Smithfield EC1 🚇 Barbican ⏰ 8:30am-5pm Mon-Fri (to 4pm mid-Nov-mid-Feb), 10:30am-4pm Sat, 8:30am-8pm Sun 🌐 greatstbarts.com

One of London's oldest churches, St Bart's was founded in 1123 by the monk Rahere, whose tomb is inside. A courtier of Henry I, he dreamed that the saint saved him from a winged monster.

The 13th-century arch used to be the door; the gatehouse above it is from a later period. The crossing and chancel are original, with fine Norman detailing. There are also some Tudor monuments. In the south transept is a gilded statue of St Bartholomew by Damien Hirst. In 1725, US statesman Benjamin Franklin worked for a printer in the Lady Chapel. The church also featured in the films *Four Weddings and a Funeral*, *Shakespeare in Love* and *The Other Boleyn Girl*.

The Sky Garden

📍 N5 🏛 20 Fenchurch St EC3 🚇 Bank, Monument ⏰ 10am-6pm Mon-Fri (last adm: 5pm), 11am-9pm Sat & Sun (last adm: 8pm) 🌐 skygarden. london

The Rafael Viñoly-designed 20 Fenchurch Street is commonly known as the "Walkie-Talkie", thanks to its unusual shape. Not without controversy (its shape and position make it particularly obtrusive on the city skyline), it is one of few skyscrapers with free public access, provided that you book ahead for the Sky Garden, a three-level viewing deck. Tickets are released each Monday for the following week and go quickly. There are also bars and restaurants. This is a perfect place from which to view London's other mega-structures. To the south is the Shard; north are Tower 42, the "Gherkin" and the Leadenhall Building, aka the "Cheesegrater", "The Scalpel" and 22 Bishopsgate, the city's *tallest skyscraper*.

St Katharine Docks
📍 O6 🏠 E1 🚇 Tower Hill
🌐 skdocks.co.uk

This most central of all London's docks was designed by Thomas Telford and opened in 1828 on the site of St Katharine's Hospital. Commodities as diverse as tea, marble and live turtles (turtle soup was a Victorian delicacy) were unloaded here. During the 19th and early 20th centuries, the docks flourished, but by the mid-20th century, cargo ships were delivering their wares in massive containers. The old docks became too small and closed in 1968. The redevelopment of St Katharine's has been one of the City's most successful –the old warehouse buildings have shops and restaurants on their ground floors, and offices above. In front is a marina, and there are other entertainment facilities. The dock is well worth wandering through after visiting the Tower or Tower Bridge. A weekly street food market is held here on Saturdays from 11am to 3pm.

Guildhall
📍 M4 🏠 Guildhall Yard EC2 🚇 St Paul's 🚇 Great Hall: 10am–4.30pm Mon-Sat, (daily May–Sep)
🕐 1 Jan, 25 & 26 Dec, occasionally for events
🌐 guildhall.cityoflondon.gov.uk

Guildhall has been the administrative centre of the City for at least 800 years. For centuries its Great Hall was used for trials, and many people were condemned to death here, including Henry Garnet, one of the Gunpowder Plot conspirators. Overlooking the Great Hall at one end are the figures of legendary giants Gog and Magog, the guardians of the City, while statues of notable figures such as Churchill and Nelson line its 46-m- (150-ft-) long sides. Each year, a few days after the Lord Mayor's parade, the prime minister addresses a banquet here.

On the south side of Guildhall Yard is a Wren-designed church, St Lawrence Jewry, while on the east side is the Guildhall Art Gallery. It houses the studio collection of 20th-century artist Sir Matthew Smith, portraits from the 16th century to the present day, 18th-century works including John Singleton Copley's *Defeat of the Floating Batteries at Gibraltar*, and numerous Victorian works. In 1988, the foundations of a Roman amphitheatre were discovered beneath the gallery. Built in AD 70 and with a capacity of about 6,000 spectators, the arena would have hosted animal hunts, executions and gladiatorial combat. Public access to the atmospheric ruins is through the art gallery.

DRINK

Merchant House
Hidden away down an alley, this basement bar and lounge serves up exceptional cocktails, which evoke the Empire. The Brig, a private bar inside seating just 2-4 people, can be hired.

📍 M5 🏠 13 Well Court, off Bow Lane EC4 🌐 merchant house.bar

SHOREDITCH AND SPITALFIELDS

These districts have attracted and spawned a once cutting-edge, much caricatured and now simply trendy local population. Though gentrification has firmly set in there is still an alluring energy here, particularly in lively Shoreditch. It's not entirely hipster-centric though, with Brick Lane home to a large Bangladeshi community, and markets like Old Spitalfields and Columbia Road continuing traditions that stretch way back beyond the latest incarnation of the neighbourhood.

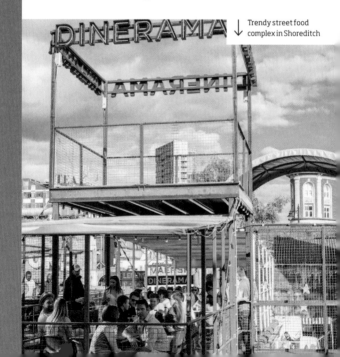

↓ Trendy street food complex in Shoreditch

Independent traders with
their wares on display at
Old Spitalfields Market

activities to keep children
amused, including story-
telling, arts and crafts
workshops, and fun trails.

EXPERIENCE

Old Spitalfields Market

📍 03 🏠 16 Horner Sq E1
🚇 Liverpool St, Aldgate
🕐 Market stalls: 10am-
6pm daily (till 5pm Sun),
7am-6pm Thu
🌐 oldspitalfields
market.com

Produce has been traded
at Spitalfields Market since
1682, though the original
covered market buildings
date to 1887. The vegetable
market finally moved out
in 1991, after which today's
version of the market –
known for antiques, fashion,
bric-a-brac and crafts stalls –
started to take shape. Today
the market space is a mix
of restaurants, shops and
traditional market stalls. It is
open every day; Thursdays
are good for antiques and
collectibles, and every other
Friday for vinyl records, but
it is on Sundays that the
crowds really arrive, in
search of vintage clothing
and unique items. This is
also a major foodie destination, with superb street
food from top names, both
global and local – from
Pacific pokè and Burmese
tea leaf salad to East Anglian
oysters and the unrivalled
Reuben sandwich from the
iconic Monty's Deli.

V&A Museum of Childhood

📍 02 🏠 Cambridge Heath
Rd E2 🚇 Bethnal Green
🕐 10am-5:45pm daily
🌐 vam.ac.uk/moc

With an amazing array of
toys, games, puzzles, lavish
dolls' houses, model train
sets, furniture and costumes,
dating from the 16th century
up to the present day, this
museum has the largest
collection of childhood-
related objects in the UK.
There are plenty of

Petticoat Lane

📍 04 🏠 Middlesex St E1
🚇 Aldgate East, Aldgate,
Liverpool St 🕐 9am-
2pm Sun (main market);
(smaller market on
Wentworth St)

During the prudish Victorian
era, the name of this street,
long famous for its market,
was changed to the more
respectable but colourless
Middlesex Street. That is still
its official designation, but
the old name, derived from
the petticoats and lace sold
here by the Huguenots who
came from France, has stuck,
and is now applied to the
market held every Sunday
morning in this and the
surrounding streets. Though
the street is not particularly
attractive, the lively market
creates plenty of atmosphere.
A great variety of goods are
sold, but there is still a bias
towards clothing, especially
leather coats. It's a noisy and
cheerful scene, with Cockney
stallholders making use of
their wit to attract custom.
There are scores of snack
bars for pitstops.

Hoxton

📍N2 🏠N1, E2 🚇Old St

Hoxton, at the heart of hipster London, is a loosely defined district that revolves around its two main streets: Old Street and Kingsland Road. This once-gritty landscape of Victorian warehouses is now home to trendy places to eat, increasingly pricey clothes stores and a significant percentage of the city's newer street art. The converted warehouses house some of the city's most rambunctious nightlife, with clubs and bars radiating out from the Shoreditch High Street and Old Street junction, some of them on neatly proportioned Hoxton Square, just behind Old Street.

Dennis Severs' House

📍03 🏠18 Folgate St E1 🚇Liverpool St 🕐Noon-2pm & 5-9pm Mon, 5-9pm Wed & Fri, noon-4pm Sun 🌐dennissevershouse. co.uk

At No 18 Folgate Street, built in 1724, the late designer and performer Dennis Severs re-created a historical interior that takes you on a journey from the 17th to the 19th centuries. It offers what he called "an adventure of the imagination... a visit to a time-mode rather than... merely a look at a house".

The rooms are like a series of *tableaux vivants*, as if the occupants had simply left for a moment. There is bread on the plates, wine in the glasses, fruit in the bowl; the candles flicker and horses' hooves are heard clattering on the cobbles outside.

This highly theatrical experience is far removed from the usual museum re-creations, and the house is particularly atmospheric on the regular "Silent Night" evenings (book ahead) and at Christmas. Praised by many, including artist David Hockney, it is truly unique. The house's motto is "You either see it or you don't."

Around the corner on Elder Street are two of London's earliest surviving terraces, where several Georgian red-brick houses have been carefully restored.

↑ Beautiful blooms at the Columbia Road flower market

Columbia Road Market

📍02 🏠Columbia Rd E2 🚇Hoxton 🕐8am-3pm Sun 🌐columbia road.info

A visit to this flower and plant market is one of the most delightful things to do on a Sunday morning in London, whether you want to take advantage of the exotic species on offer or not – though it's hard to resist, as prices are competitive and the range impressive. Set in a well-preserved street of small Victorian shops, it is a lively, sweet-smelling and colourful affair. Apart from the stalls, there are several shops selling, among other things, home-made bread and farmhouse cheeses, antiques and interesting objects, many flower related. There are also cafés, a tapas bar and pubs to refuel at along the street. Visit early to miss the crowds.

Whitechapel Gallery

📍04 🏠77-82 Whitechapel High St E1 🚇Aldgate East, Aldgate 🕐11am-6pm Tue-Sun (to 9pm Thu) 📅1 Jan, 24-26 Dec 🌐whitechapel gallery.org

A striking Art Nouveau façade by C Harrison Townsend fronts this light, airy gallery, founded in 1901 and later expanded in the 1980s and again in 2007–9. Situated close to Brick Lane and the area's burgeoning art scene, this independent gallery was founded with the aim of bringing great art to the people of east London. Today it enjoys an international reputation for high-quality shows of major contemporary artists and for events, talks, live performances, films and art-themed evenings (especially on the first Thursday of each month, when many galleries in the area open late).

In the 1950s and 1960s, the likes of Jackson Pollock, Anthony Caro, Mark Rothko, Robert Rauschenberg and John Hoyland all displayed their work in the gallery. In 1970 David Hockney's first exhibition was held here. The gallery has a well-stocked arts bookshop and a relaxed café which on Thursday evenings becomes a popular wine bar. There is an entry charge for some special exhibitions.

Brick Lane

📍03 🏠E1 🚇Liverpool St, Aldgate East 🚌Shoreditch High St 🕐Market: 10am–5pm Sun 🌐visitbricklane.org

Once a lane running through brickfields, Brick Lane has long been synonymous with the area's British-Bangladeshi community. Now their curry houses sit next to hip galleries and quirky boutiques. Shops and houses, some dating from the 18th century, have seen immigrants of many nationalities, and ethnic foods, spices, silks and saris are all on sale here. In the 19th century this was mainly a Jewish quarter, and some Jewish shops remain, most famously a 24-hour bagel shop at No 159. On Sundays, a large market is held here and in the surrounding streets. Towards the northern end of Brick Lane is the Old Truman Brewery, home to a mix of bars, shops and stalls: separate markets at weekends sell food, vintage clothes and new fashion.

EAT

Dinerama

Best spot for street food after dark, this old truck depot offers craft beer and cocktails.

📍N3 🏠19 Great Eastern St EC2 🕐Wed-Sat

💷💷💷

The Brick Lane Food Hall

Treats from Poland, Ethiopia, Japan, Korea and more inside a red-brick warehouse.

📍03 🏠Old Truman Brewery, Brick Lane E1 🕐Sat & Sun

💷💷💷

Sunday Upmarket

International street food is found among artsy stalls.

📍03 🏠Old Truman Brewery, Brick Lane E1 🕐Sun

💷💷💷

SOUTHWARK AND BANKSIDE

Over the river from the City, Bankside, in the borough of Southwark, contains some of the most popular tourist attractions on the Thames. Tate Modern and Shakespeare's Globe along with waterside restaurants, pubs and Borough Market keep this stretch of the Thames Path happily congested most days. The recently developed area emanating out from London Bridge station has plenty of new places to eat, a few of them in Western Europe's tallest building, the Shard.

Charcuterie and cheese at the French Comte in Borough Market ↓

TATE MODERN

📍L6 🏠Bankside SE1 🚇Blackfriars, Southwark
🚆Blackfriars 🕐10am-6pm Sun-Thu, 10am-10pm
Fri & Sat 🚫24-26 Dec 🌐tate.org.uk

Looming over the southern bank of the Thames, Tate Modern, housed in the converted Bankside power station, holds one of the world's premier collections of contemporary art. With an ever-changing roster of exhibitions, it is London's most visited gallery.

Opened to coincide with the new millennium, this Goliath of a gallery boasts a collection of over 70,000 works of modern art, featuring paintings and sculptures by some of the most significant artists of the 20th and 21st centuries, Pablo Picasso, Salvador Dalí, Mark Rothko and Francis Bacon among them. Lesser known artists and less mainstream media also abound, with pieces composed of bottle tops or, most famously, a porcelain urinal, in the guise of Marcel Duchamp's notorious *Fountain*. The focal point of the building is the awesome Turbine Hall, which is often filled by a specially commissioned work. Other exhibition spaces, including the galleries of the towering Blavatnik Building, feature collections on a single theme or hugely popular temporary shows.

INTERACTIVE ART

Tate Modern has created a series of interactive activities and experiences under its Bloomberg Connects umbrella. These products, including the Tate app, the digital Drawing Bar and the digital gallery, in which you can immerse yourself in the studios and cities of artists, enable members of the public to actively connect with art, artists and other visitors. The award-winning handheld multimedia guides present audio commentary alongside images, film clips and games.

→ The striking chimney of Tate Modern reveals the building's former role as a power station; *One Two Three Swing!*, an installation by SUPERFLEX *(inset)*

SHAKESPEARE'S GLOBE

📍L5 🏠New Globe Walk SE1 🚇Blackfriars, London Bridge, Mansion House 🕐Tours & exhibition: 9am–5pm 🚫24 & 26 Dec
🌐shakespearesglobe.com

To see a Shakespeare play at the reconstructed Globe is a magical experience. Time-travel to the 1600s and watch Romeo woo Juliet, Beatrice and Benedick squabble, and Hamlet seek revenge.

Built along the south bank of the Thames, Shakespeare's Globe is a fine reconstruction of the Elizabethan theatre where many of the famous playwright's works were first performed. The circular wooden structure is open in the middle, leaving some of the audience exposed to the elements. Those holding seated tickets enjoy a roof over their heads. Performances (staged from late April until mid-October) are thrilling, with first-rate acting. A second theatre, the Sam Wanamaker Playhouse, is a splendidly atmospheric, candlelit reproduction of a Jacobean indoor theatre, with performances year-round. The Globe also houses an exhibition telling the history of Elizabethan theatre in Southwark, the process of building the Globe and the exquisite costumes made for shows there. You can also listen to classic performances of speeches from Shakespeare's works.

> 💬 INSIDER TIP
> **Wrap Up**
>
> Got tickets? Dress warmly: plays tend to run for several hours and even during the summer months London evenings can be very cool.

Did You Know?

The Taming of the Shrew is considered Shakespeare's first play, written before 1592.

→

The theatre, built with green oak beams and lime plaster to replicate the 1599 original

EXPERIENCE MORE

The Old Operating Theatre

📍 M6 🏠 9a St Thomas St
SE1 🚇 London Bridge
🕐 10:30am–5pm
Tue–Sun, 2–5pm Mon
🚫 24–26 & 31 Dec, 1 Jan
🌐 oldoperating
theatre.com

St Thomas' Hospital, one of the oldest in Britain, stood here from its foundation in the 12th century until it was moved west in 1862. At this time, nearly all of its buildings were demolished in order to make way for the railways. The women's operating theatre survived only because it had been constructed in a garret over the hospital church.

The UK's oldest operating theatre, dating from 1822, it remained forgotten until the 1950s. It has now been fitted out just as it would have been in the early 19th century, before the discovery of either antiseptics or anaesthetics. Another section of the garret, which was once used by the hospital apothecary to store herbs, has a collection of traditional herbs and remedies, plus displays of antiquated medicines.

As the museum is upstairs in a historic building, wheelchair access is problematic.

↑ Southwark's busy Borough Market and surrounding area

Borough Market

📍 M6 🏠 8 Southwark St
SE1 🚇 London Bridge
🕐 10am–5pm Wed–Thu,
10am–6pm Fri, 8am–5pm
Sat (some stalls also
10am–5pm Mon & Tue)
🌐 boroughmarket.org.uk

Borough Market has existed in some form or another for over a thousand years. It moved to its current position in 1756 and became one of Britain's biggest fruit and vegetable markets after the arrival of the railways in the 19th century. Today, it's an extremely popular fine food market (beware: the crowds can be huge, especially on Fridays and Saturdays), known for gourmet goods, as well as quality fruit and vegetables, and organic meat, fish and dairy produce. A number of hot food stalls, selling a tempting array of dishes from around the world, also share the space. Food demonstrations take place in the glass atrium on Borough High Street on Thursdays and Fridays. The specialist food shops and pubs on the streets around the market are also well worth checking out.

DRINK

The George

The only remaining galleried coaching inn in London, with seating outside in the courtyard.

📍 M6 🏠 75–77
Borough High St SE1
🌐 greene
king-pubs.co.uk

The Anchor

Ales have been quaffed here for centuries. The present 18th-century premises has a terrace by the river.

📍 M6 🏠 34 Park St
SE1 🌐 greeneking-
pubs.co.uk

Bermondsey Street

📍 N7 🏠 SE1 🚇 London Bridge, Borough

Bermondsey's winding streets still hold traces of its past in the form of medieval, 18th-century and Victorian buildings. Today, Bermondsey Street is home to galleries, coffee shops and a few great restaurants. The area is also famous for its antiques market, held in Bermondsey Square at the bottom end of the street. Each Friday morning from 6am, seriously committed antiques dealers trade their latest acquisitions, and the best bargains tend to go before most people are even awake.

The Fashion and Textile Museum at No 83 puts on a programme of exhibitions covering all aspects of fashion and design, and also runs an education programme. Further along the street, White Cube Bermondsey is a major space for international contemporary art.

City Hall

📍 O6 🏠 The Queen's Walk SE1 🚇 London Bridge 🕒 8:30am-6pm Mon-Thu, 8:30am-5:30pm Fri 🌐 london.gov.uk/about-us

The Norman Foster–designed domed glass building just by Tower Bridge is the headquarters for London's mayor and the Greater London Authority. Anyone can visit the building and head up the walkway to the second floor to look in on the assembly chamber, or sit in on Mayor's Question Time, when assembly members interrogate the mayor on London issues; this takes place ten times a year on Wednesday mornings (check website for dates). On the lower ground floor are temporary exhibitions and a café. Outside, the stone amphitheatre known as the Scoop hosts free events in summer, including plays, music and screenings.

Clink Prison Museum

📍 M6 🏠 1 Clink St SE1 🚇 London Bridge 🕒 Jul-Sep: 10am-9pm daily; Oct-Jun: 10am-6pm Mon-Fri, 10am-7:30pm Sat & Sun 🌐 clink.co.uk

The prison that was once located here was founded in the 12th century. It was owned by successive Bishops of Winchester, who lived in the adjoining palace, of which all that now remains is a lovely rose window on Clink Street.

During the 15th century, the prison became known as the "Clink", and this has become a British slang term for any prison or jail cell. It closed down in 1780.

The museum alongside the remains of the palace illustrates the history of the prison. Tales are told of the inmates incarcerated here, including prostitutes, debtors, and priests imprisoned by the bishop as heretics. Visitors can handle instruments of torture that leave little to the imagination – a trip here is not for the faint-hearted.

The Shard

📍 N6 🏠 London Bridge St 🚇 London Bridge 🕒 The View from the Shard: 10am-10pm daily; last adm 1 hour before closing 🌐 theviewfromtheshard.com

Designed by Renzo Piano, the Shard is the tallest building in western Europe.

→

The Shard, rising up behind the visor-shaped City Hall

At 310 m (1,016 ft) high with a crystalline façade, the 95-storey tower houses offices, restaurants – several with incredible views across the city – a five-star hotel, exclusive apartments and the country's highest observation gallery, the View from the Shard. Take a high-speed lift from the entrance on Joiner Street to the top of the building for spectacular, unobstructed views of the capital. There are two viewing floors, the higher of which is right among the "shards" with the breeze blowing overhead.

HMS Belfast

📍 N6 🏠 The Queen's Walk SE1 🚇 London Bridge, Tower Hill 🕐 Mar–Oct: 10am–6pm daily (last adm: 5pm); Nov–Feb: 10am–5pm (last adm: 4pm) 📅 24–26 Dec 🌐 iwm.org.uk/visits/hms-belfast

Launched in 1938 to serve in World War II,

HMS *Belfast* was instrumental in the destruction of the German battle cruiser *Scharnhorst* in the Battle of North Cape, and also played a role in the Normandy landings. After the war, the battle cruiser was sent to work for the United Nations during the Korean War, and remained in service with the Royal Navy until 1965.

The only surviving World War II cruiser, it has been used as a floating naval museum since 1971. Ideal for children and adults alike, visitors can climb down ladders to the engine room 4.5 m (15 ft) below sea level, and experience what it was like in the gun turrets during a battle. Exhibits also explore the ship's history post-World War II, including during the Cold War.

EAT

Roast
Traditional British food at its best in a smart dining room overlooking Borough Market.

📍 M6 🏠 The Floral Hall, Stoney St SE1 🌐 roast-restaurant.com

£ £ £

Flat Iron Square
A sociable hub for street food and quality independent fast-food restaurants in the railway arches near Borough Market.

📍 M6 🏠 68 Union St SE1 🌐 flatironsquare.co.uk

£ £ £

The Garrison
The seasonal British menu served here is a mixture of the creatively modern and the satisfyingly traditional.

📍 N7 🏠 99–101 Bermondsey St SE1 🌐 thegarrison.co.uk

£ £ £

SOUTH BANK

At night this is the liveliest part of the river, but it is cultural institutions rather than nightclubs that draw in the after-dark crowds. The Southbank Centre's concert halls and gallery alongside the National Theatre and British Film Institute form a striking line-up of architecture along the river. Any gaps are filled mostly with mediocre chain restaurants, though bookstalls, a skate park and a food market provide a more homespun angle. Always busy in the daytime too, the views from the South Bank promenade – and from atop the London Eye – have cemented it as one of London's must-visit areas.

↓ Royal Festival Hall
  on the South Bank

←
Crowds enjoying the sun outside the Queen Elizabeth Hall

SOUTHBANK CENTRE

📍J6 🏠Belvedere Rd, South Bank SE1 🚇Waterloo, Embankment 🚆Waterloo, Waterloo East, Charing Cross 🚢Festival Pier, London Eye Pier, Mon-Fri
🌐southbankcentre.co.uk

With a major art gallery and three world-class auditoriums for music, dance and other events lined up along the river, the Southbank Centre is one of London's pre-eminent cultural and performance venues.

London's high-profile, much-respected and visited multi-dimensional arts centre takes centre stage among the other great arts institutions on the South Bank: the National Theatre and the British Film Institute. The Southbank Centre itself comprises four main venues: the Royal Festival Hall, the Hayward Gallery, the Queen Elizabeth Hall and the Purcell Room. The centre's always buzzing, with bustling bars and restaurants slotted into and between the terraces, platforms, walkways and rooftops of this concrete complex. There are always innumerable visitors making their way to performances, primarily of classical music but also of opera, folk, world music and all kinds of contemporary leftfield genres. Comedy, talks and dance all feature too, while there is a multitude of regular festivals, seasons and weekends staged here, including the London Jazz Festival, Women of the World (WOW) Festival, the London Literature Festival and Meltdown.

EAT

Southbank Centre Food Market

This excellent little food market is located to the rear of the Royal Festival Hall. A wide range of street eats is available, from pizzas and curries to Korean BBQ and Ethiopian vegan food, as well as treats to take home, like wine, cheese and jam.

🕐Noon-8pm Fri, 11am-8pm Sat & noon-6pm Sun

£££

Did You Know?

The foundation stone of Royal Festival Hall was laid in 1949 by Prime Minister Clement Attlee.

↑ The museum housed in a former hospital; military aircraft on display (inset)

IMPERIAL WAR MUSEUM

📍K8 🏛Lambeth Rd SE1 ⊖Waterloo, Lambeth North, Elephant & Castle 🚆Waterloo, Elephant & Castle 🕙10am–6pm daily (last admission to the Holocaust Gallery at 5:30pm) 📞24–26 Dec 🌐iwm.org.uk

With great creativity and sensitivity, the immersive exhibitions at the terrific Imperial War Museum provide a fascinating insight into the history of war and themes of conflict.

 INSIDER TIP
Get a Guide

There is a guide book to the museum aimed specifically at children aged 7 and above. There are also daily 40-minute tours (£10, children £5) at 11am and 3pm that introduce the museum's collections. Tickets must be bought in person.

Inevitably the two World Wars feature heavily at the Imperial War Museum, but they are covered in innovative ways. In the First World War Galleries, there are original exhibits such as a recreated trench, while some of the most fascinating World War II exhibits relate more to the impact on the lives of people at home than to the business of fighting. One display focuses on the experiences of a London family, including the effects of food rationing and regular air raids. The Holocaust Exhibition is a particularly poignant experience, while other highly original permanent displays include Curiosities of War, which is full of unexpected items such as a wooden training horse from World War I. More conventionally, there are tanks, artillery and aircraft, including a Mark 1 Spitfire and a Harrier jet, on show in the main atrium.

THE LONDON EYE

◨ J6 ◨ Jubilee Gardens SE1 ◨ Waterloo, Westminster ◨ From 10am daily; closing times between 6pm and 8:30pm; check website for details ◨ Two weeks in Jan for maintenance ◨ londoneye.com

Stunning views of London's historic skyline can be had from the glass capsules of the city's famous ferris wheel, the London Eye. Situated right beside the River Thames, visitors enjoy a 360-degree view of the city.

The London Eye is a 135-m- (443-ft-) high observation wheel. Opened in 2000 as part of London's millennium celebrations, it immediately became one of the city's most recognizable landmarks, notable not only for its size, but for its circularity amid the block-shaped buildings flanking it. Thirty-two capsules, each holding up to 25 people, take a gentle 30-minute round trip. On a clear day, the Eye affords a 40-km (25-mile) view over the capital in all directions and out to the countryside beyond.

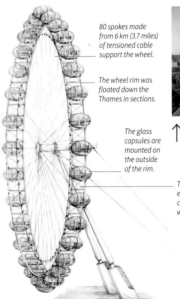

80 spokes made from 6 km (3.7 miles) of tensioned cable support the wheel.

The wheel rim was floated down the Thames in sections.

The glass capsules are mounted on the outside of the rim.

The Eye turns slowly enough that the capsules are boarded while they are moving.

↑ A capsule mid-tour with unimpeded views of the city

← Illustration of the London Eye, on the South Bank

EXPERIENCE MORE

Lambeth Palace

📍 J8 🏛 SE1
🚇 Lambeth North,
Westminster, Waterloo,
Vauxhall
🎫 For tours only
🌐 archbishopof
canterbury.org

This Grade I–listed palace
has housed Archbishops of
Canterbury since the 13th
century and today remains
the archbishop's official
London residence. The
chapel and its undercroft
contain elements from
the 13th century, but a
large part of the rest of
the building is far more
recent. It has been fre-
quently restored, including
by Edward Blore in 1828.
The Tudor gatehouse dates
from 1485 and is one of
the city's most familiar
riverside landmarks.

The garden, planted
with many mature trees,
is open on the first
Friday of the month in
summer, while you can
visit the palace year-
round by pre-booking a
place on a guided tour
(check website).

Until the first
Westminster Bridge was
built, the horse ferry that
operated between here
and Millbank was a principal river crossing. The
revenues from this ferry
went to the archbishop.

The Old Vic

📍 K7 🏛 Waterloo Rd SE1
🚇 Waterloo 🎫 For
performances and tours
🌐 oldvictheatre.com

This splendid building dates
back to 1818 and changed
its name to the Royal
Victoria in 1833 in honour of
the future queen. The
theatre became a centre for
music hall, the immensely
popular Victorian entertainment. In 1912, Lillian Baylis
became manager and from
1914 to 1923 staged all of
Shakespeare's plays here.
The National Theatre,
founded in the 1960s, was
formerly based at this site.
In 2003 the Old Vic Theatre
Company was set up as the
resident company. Though
tickets are pricey, there are
cheap seats for younger
people. Theatre tours (which
can be booked online) are
fascinating, full of backstage
snippets and anecdotes.

Gabriel's Wharf

📍 K6 🏛 56 Upper Ground
SE1 🚇 Waterloo

This pleasant enclave of
boutiques, craft shops and
cafés was the product of a
long and stormy debate
over the future of what was
once an industrial riverside
area. Residents of Waterloo
strongly opposed various
schemes for office develop-

ments before a community
association was able to
acquire the site in 1984 and
build cooperative housing.

Adjoining the market
area is a small public garden
with grass to sit on and a
river pier with fine views of
the City. The Oxo Tower to
the east was adapted from
an older power station in
1928 to surreptitiously
advertise a well-known
meat extract by means of
its window shapes. It now
houses galleries and design
shops on the lower floors
and a bar, restaurant and
brasserie on the top floor.

National Theatre

📍 K6 🏛 South Bank SE1
🚇 Waterloo ⏰ 9:30am–
11pm Mon-Sat (Sherling
Walkway closes 7:30pm)
🚫 24 & 25 Dec 🌐 national
theatre.org.uk

Even if you don't want to
see a play, this complex is
worth a visit, especially for a
backstage tour. These are
offered Monday to Saturday,
and it is advisable to book

← The controversial Brutalist architecture of the National Theatre

in advance. You can also get a glimpse of the backstage area from the Sherling High-Level Walkway (entrance near the Dorfman Theatre), which runs above the prop-building areas.

Sir Denys Lasdun's building opened in 1976 after 200 years of debate: should there be a national theatre and, if so, where? The theatre company was formed in 1963, under Laurence (later Lord) Olivier. The largest of the three theatres is named after him; the others are the Dorfman and the Lyttleton. Prestigious productions are streamed live to theatres and cinemas all over the UK, and occasionally the world, via the National Theatre Live initiative, as well as taken on tours.

Sea Life London Aquarium

📍 J7 🏛 County Hall, Westminster Bridge Rd SE1 🚇 Waterloo ⏰ 10am-6pm Mon-Fri, 9:30am-7pm Sat, Sun & public hols (last adm: 6pm) 🌐 visitsealife.com/london

Once the home of London's elected government, County

Hall now houses the Sea Life London Aquarium and London Dungeon, alongside a hotel, restaurants and other themed attractions.

The aquarium is home to myriad aquatic species, such as stingrays, turtles, jellyfish, starfish and penguins. There's a 25-m (82-ft) glass tunnel walkway through a tropical ocean environment, and a large tank housing numerous shark species, which you can view from several levels. Book ahead to guarantee entry and skip large queues.

London Dungeon

📍 J7 🏛 County Hall, Westminster Bridge Rd SE1 🚇 Waterloo ⏰ 10am-5pm Mon-Fri & Sun (from 11am Thu), 10am-6pm Sat; extended hours in school holidays 🌐 thedungeons.com

This scary attraction is a great hit with older children. Illustrating the most bloodthirsty events in British history with live actors and special effects, the dungeon plays strictly for terror, and screams abound during the 90-minute tour. Gory scenes recount tales of such characters as Guy Fawkes and Jack the Ripper. Don't miss the Tyrant Boat Ride along a black River Thames to find out what happened to Tudor queen Anne Boleyn and her co-conspirators.

Museum of Garden History

📍 J8 🏛 Lambeth Palace Rd SE1 🚇 Waterloo, Lambeth North, Westminster ⏰ 10:30am-5pm Sun-Fri, 10:30-4pm Sat 🚫 First Mon of month; 23 Dec-2 Jan 🌐 gardenmuseum.org.uk

The world's first museum of garden history is housed in the restored church of St Mary of Lambeth Palace, where it is set around a central knot garden. In the grounds are the tombs of John Tradescant, father and son, who, as well as being gardeners to Charles I and Charles II, were adventurous plant hunters. The tomb of William Bligh of HMS *Bounty*, the ship set adrift in the Pacific Ocean after the fateful mutiny, can also be seen here. Coincidentally, his vessel had been on a plant-collecting voyage.

The museum presents a history of gardening in Britain, including objects collected by the Tradescants, and an archive of garden design. It also runs a programme of exhibitions and events, and has a shop and café. During renovations in 2017, which created a new garden and opened up the church tower for the first time, a vault was discovered with 30 lead coffins.

CHELSEA AND BATTERSEA

Sitting on opposite sides of the Thames are wealthy Chelsea and energetic Battersea. Flashy sedans and 4WD vehicles, known locally as Chelsea tractors, ply Chelsea's main shopping street, King's Road, where upmarket fashion boutiques sit next door to more humdrum high-street stores. Away from King's Road the area is largely residential, though there are some decent pubs, worthwhile museums and gardens. The glorious park, trendy shops and varied restaurants of Battersea are a welcome retreat from the touristy sights of central London.

↓ The Peace Pagoda in Battersea Park

↑ *Untitled* by Maha Mullah in the Champagne Life exhibition at the Saatchi Gallery

EXPERIENCE

Saatchi Gallery

📍 F9 🏠 Duke of York's HQ, King's Rd SW3
🚇 Sloane Square
🕐 10am–6pm daily during exhibitions (last adm: 5:30pm) 🔒 For private events
🌐 saatchigallery.com

Set up by advertising mogul Charles Saatchi in order to showcase his impressive contemporary art acquisitions, the Saatchi Gallery has moved location several times in London. Now, however, it is firmly established in Chelsea at the Duke of York's Headquarters building, which dates from 1801. Saatchi is perhaps best known for his espousal, in the 1980s and 1990s, of the Young British Artists movement led by Damien Hirst. Today, the exhibitions of contemporary art staged here are wide-ranging and international in scope, covering everything from new Chinese artists to fashion illustration and Pop Art.

Chelsea Physic Garden

📍 E10 🏠 66 Royal Hospital Rd SW3
🚇 Sloane Square 🕐 Apr–Oct: 11am–6pm Mon–Fri & Sun; Nov–Mar: 11am–4pm Mon–Fri 🔒 Six weeks mid-Dec-Jan 🌐 chelsea physicgarden.co.uk

Established by the Society of Apothecaries in 1673 to study plants for medicinal use, this garden was saved from closure in 1722 by a gift from Sir Hans Sloane, whose statue adorns it. New varieties nurtured in its glasshouses have included cotton sent to the plantations of the southern United States. Visitors to London's oldest botanic garden can see ancient trees and one of Britain's first rock gardens, installed in 1772.

King's Road

📍 E9 🏠 SW3 and SW10
🚇 Sloane Square

This is Chelsea's central artery, with a wealth of upmarket high-street shops and smaller boutiques. The miniskirt revolution of the 1960s – the birth of so-called "Swinging London" – began here, with Mary Quant's first shop, Bazaar, and so have many subsequent style trends, perhaps the most famous of them being punk.

Look out for the Pheasantry at No 152, with its columns and statuary. Built in 1881 as the shopfront of a furniture-maker's premises, it now con ceals a pizza restaurant.

At the top of King's Road is attractive 18th-century Sloane Square, named after Sir Hans Sloane, the wealthy physician and collector who bought the manor of Chelsea in 1712. On the east side is the Royal Court Theatre, which for over a century has fostered new drama.

Royal Hospital Chelsea

⊙ F9 **🏛** Royal Hospital Rd SW3 **Ⓢ** Sloane Square **🕐** Museum, chapel and Great Hall: 10am–4pm Mon–Fri (no access to Hall noon–2pm) **🔒** 2 weeks over Christmas, public hols, for functions **🌐** chelsea-pensioners.co.uk

This graceful complex was commissioned by Charles II from Christopher Wren in 1682 as a retirement home for old or wounded soldiers, who have been known as Chelsea Pensioners ever since. The hospital opened ten years later and is still home to about 300 retired soldiers, whose distinctive uniform of scarlet coat and tricorn hat dates from the 17th century. The Pensioners lead guided tours of the hospital, but only for prebooked groups.

Flanking the northern entrance are Wren's two main public rooms: the chapel, notable for its wonderful simplicity, and the panelled Great Hall. A small museum covers the history of the Chelsea Pensioners.

A statue of Charles II by Grinling Gibbons is to be found on the terrace outside, from where there is a fine view of Battersea Power Station across the river.

Battersea Park

⊙ F10 **🏛** Albert Bridge Rd SW11 **Ⓢ** Sloane Square then bus 137 **🚂** Battersea Park **🕐** 6:30am–10:30pm daily **🌐** wandsworth.gov.uk/batterseapark

This was the second public park created to relieve the growing urban stresses of Victorian Londoners – the first was Victoria Park in the East End. It opened in 1858 on the former Battersea Fields, a swampy area notorious for vice centred on the Old Red House, a disreputable pub. The new park was immediately popular, especially for its man-made boating lake, with its romantic rocks, gardens and waterfalls. In 1985, the Peace Pagoda was unveiled – a 35-m- (100-ft-) high monument built by Japanese Buddhist nuns and monks and presented to the park as a gift. There is also an excellent children's zoo (entry fee), a playground, sports activities and an art gallery, the Pumphouse.

Circus West Village

⊙ G10 **🏛** Battersea Power Station **Ⓢ** Sloane Sq then bus 452 or 137 **🚂** Battersea Power Station **🌐** battersea powerstation.co.uk

Most easily reached by boat, Circus West is the first stage of the gargantuan redevelopment of Battersea Power Station, part of the regeneration of riverside land stretching between Battersea Park and Vauxhall in between the towering power station and the train lines heading into Victoria Station. Its ongoing development, though certainly commercially driven, just about bridges the gap between the independent

The Great Hall at the Royal Hospital Chelsea, laid out for the Pensioners' lunch

and corporate business worlds. An interesting mix of restaurants, bars and shops have been installed inside the railway arches and by the new-builds gathering around the site, including a brewpub, cinema and the Village Hall performance venue.

Chelsea Harbour
🅟 C10 🏠 SW10
🄴 Fulham Broadway
🚇 Imperial Wharf

This is an impressive development of modern apartments, shops, offices, restaurants, a hotel and a marina. It is near the site of Cremorne Pleasure Gardens, which closed in 1877 after more than 40 years as a venue for dances and circuses. The centrepiece of the harbour is the Belvedere, a 20-storey apartment tower with an external glass lift and a pyramid roof, topped with a golden ball on a rod that rises and falls with the tide.

Carlyle's House
🅟 D10 🏠 24 Cheyne Row SW3 🄴 Sloane Square, South Kensington
🕒 Mar–Oct: 11am–5pm Wed–Sun 🌐 national trust.org.uk

The historian Thomas Carlyle moved into this modest 18th-century house in 1834, and wrote many of his best-known books here, notably *The French Revolution*. His presence at this address made Chelsea more fashionable and the house became a mecca for literary figures, including novelists Charles Dickens and William Thackeray, poet Alfred Lord Tennyson and naturalist Charles Darwin. The house has been restored and looks as it would have done during Carlyle's lifetime.

Chelsea Old Church
🅟 D10 🏠 64 Cheyne Walk SW3 🄴 Sloane Square, South Kensington
🕒 2–4pm Tue–Thu 🌐 chelseaoldchurch. org.uk

Rebuilt after World War II, this square-towered building is a careful replica of the medieval church here that was largely destroyed in World War II. The glory of this church is its Tudor monuments. One to Sir Thomas More, who built a chapel here in 1528, contains an inscription he wrote (in Latin) asking to be buried next to his wife. Among other monuments is a 17th-century memorial to Lady Jane Cheyne, after whose husband Cheyne Walk was named. Outside the church is a statue in memory of More, "statesman, scholar, saint", gazing piously across the river.

EAT

Mother
The hip Copenhagen pizza joint has opened under the hangar-like railway arch in Circus West Village.

🅟 G10 🏠 Circus West Village SW11
🌐 mother restaurant.co.uk

ⓔⓔⓔ

Medlar
Refined French cuisine in a romantic, low-key environment. Good fixed-price menus.

🅟 C10 🏠 438 King's Rd SW10 🌐 medlar restaurant.co.uk

ⓔⓔⓔ

The Builder's Arms
Smart neighbourhood pub serving traditional British food. It's a congenial place to drink too.

🅟 E9 🏠 13 Britten St SW3 🌐 the buildersarms chelsea. co.uk

ⓔⓔⓔ

SOUTH KENSINGTON AND KNIGHTSBRIDGE

London's museum quarter, South Kensington is home to three of the largest and best museums in the city, exhibiting stunning natural history, science and decorative arts collections. In keeping with the spirit of learning that pervades here, the wide streets house several important royal colleges and societies. In contrast, Knightsbridge, just up the road, oozes ostentatious wealth and is the location of one of the city's most iconic department stores, Harrods.

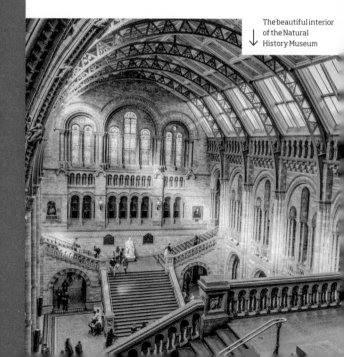

The beautiful interior of the Natural History Museum

VICTORIA AND ALBERT MUSEUM

📍D8 🏠Cromwell Road SW7 🚇South Kensington 🕙10am–5:45pm daily (till 10pm Fri) 📅24–26 Dec 🌐vam.ac.uk

Housed in Victorian splendour, as well as modern state-of-the-art galleries, the V&A is the world's leading museum of art and design, with its collection spanning 5,000 years of furniture, glass, textiles, fashion, ceramics and jewellery.

The Victoria and Albert Museum (V&A) contains one of the world's broadest collections of art and design, with exhibits ranging from early Christian devotional objects to cutting-edge furniture. Originally founded in 1852 to inspire design students as the Museum of Manufactures, it was renamed by Queen Victoria in 1899 in memory of Prince Albert. The museum has undergone extensive renovation since the early 2000s, including the opening in 2017 of a new quarter on Exhibition Road, encompassing the Sackler Courtyard and the underground Sainsbury Gallery, and an expanded Photography Centre in 2018.

↑ Large-scale works that were once part of buildings in the Medieval & Renaissance Gallery

↑ The grand Cromwell Road entrance to the V&A

GALLERY GUIDE

The V&A has six levels. Level 1 houses the China, Japan and South Asia galleries, the Fashion Gallery and the Cast Courts. The British Galleries are on Levels 2 and 4. Level 3 contains the 20th Century galleries and silver, ironwork, paintings and photography. The glass display is on Level 4. The Ceramics Galleries and Furniture are on Level 6. The fantastic European galleries from 300 to 1815 are on Level 1.

NATURAL HISTORY MUSEUM

D8 ⌂ Cromwell Rd SW7 ⊖ South Kensington 🕐 10am–5:50pm daily (till 10pm last Fri of month), last admission 5:30pm 🗓 24–26 Dec 🌐 nhm.ac.uk

A paradise for budding botanists, explorers and geologists, the superlative Natural History Museum, with its specimens, skeletons and simulators, is quite simply a national treasure and an absolute must for any visitor to the capital.

Did You Know?

Kids can spend a night at the museum at Dino Snores, a monthly event for those aged 7–11

Using interactive techniques and traditional displays, life on earth and the earth itself are vividly explained at this awe-inspiring museum. And the building that houses the vast collection is a masterpiece in itself. Founded as just several of the Victorian temples to learning, it opened in 1881 and was designed by Alfred Waterhouse using revolutionary building techniques. It is built on an iron and steel framework concealed behind arches and columns, richly decorated with sculptures of plants and animals. The museum is divided into four zones, plus the Hintze Hall, the grand centrepiece of the building dominated by a huge skeleton of a blue whale. In the Blue Zone discover Human Biology, Mammals, Dinosaurs and Images of Nature. The Green Zone has Creepy Crawlies, Fossils and the Vault. The giant escalator in the Earth Hall leads through a stunning globe to Red Zone highlights Restless Surface and Earth's Treasury. The Orange Zone includes the Darwin Centre's Cocoon and, outside, the Wildlife Garden.

The elegant museum; the huge skeleton of "Hope", the blue whale (inset). ↓

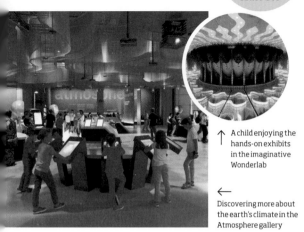

↑ A child enjoying the hands-on exhibits in the imaginative Wonderlab

← Discovering more about the earth's climate in the Atmosphere gallery

SCIENCE MUSEUM

⌖ D8 ⌂ Exhibition Rd SW7 ⊖ South Kensington ⏲ 10am–6pm daily (last entry 5:15pm) 📅 24–26 Dec Ⓦ sciencemuseum.org.uk

Centuries of continuing scientific and technological innovation lie at the heart of the Science Museum's huge collection. Discover the science fact behind science fiction and explore humanity's achievements so far – and where we might be heading next.

From steam engines to aeroengines, spacecraft to the first computers, this museum has a vast range of scientific objects. Equally important is the social context of science – what discoveries and inventions mean for day-to-day life – and the process of discovery itself. The high-tech Wellcome Wing has hands-on displays, an IMAX cinema, a 3D theatre and galleries devoted to scientific advancements.

The Science Museum's exhibits are spread over five floors. The Wellcome Wing, with four floors of interactive technology, is at the west end of the museum, accessible from the ground floor and third floor of the main building. The museum is undergoing renovations, with the spectacular new Medicine Galleries set to open on the first floor in autumn 2019; check the website for up-to-date information before you visit.

EXPERIENCE MORE

Royal College of Music

📍C7 🏛Prince Consort Rd SW7 🚇South Kensington 🌐rcm.ac.uk

Sir Arthur Blomfield designed the turreted Gothic palace, with Bavarian overtones, that has housed this disting- uished institution since 1894. Pupils have included the composers Benjamin Britten and Ralph Vaughan Williams. The RCM is currently undergoing a £40 million redevelopment, which will include two extra performance venues and a reimagined museum. Check the website for details of concerts and masterclasses hosted by the college.

Brompton Oratory

📍D8 🏛Brompton Rd SW7 🚇South Kensing- ton, Knightsbridge 🕐6:30am–8pm daily (till 7:45pm Sat, from 8am Sun) 🌐brompton oratory.co.uk

Famous for its splendid musical tradition, the Italianate Oratory is a rich (some think a little too rich) monument to the English Catholic revival of the late 19th century, established by John Henry Newman (later Cardinal Newman). The church was opened in 1884; its façade and dome were added in the 1890s, and the interior has been progressively enriched ever since. Inside, all the most eye-catching treasures predate the church – many of them were brought here from Italian churches. Giuseppe Mazzuoli carved the huge marble figures of the 12 apostles for Siena Cathedral in the late 17th century. The beautiful Lady Altar was originally created in 1693 for the Dominican church in Brescia, and the 18th- century altar in St Wilfrid's Chapel came from a church in Rochefort, Belgium.

Serpentine Galleries

📍D6 🏛Kensington Gdns W2 🚇Lancaster Gate, South Kensington 🕐10am–6pm Tue–Sun 🗓24–26 Dec & between exhibitions 🌐serpentine galleries.org

The Serpentine Gallery houses temporary exhibit- ions of major and rising contemporary artists' and architects' work, excitingly transforming its space to suit the exhibits. Every summer, a temporary pavilion is commissioned from a major architect. A second building, the

Serpentine Sackler Gallery, in a former gunpowder store a 5-minute walk away, displays similarly ambitious exhibits. An extension, designed by the late Zaha Hadid, houses the Chucs restaurant, and there is also an art bookshop.

Albert Memorial

📍C7 🏛South Carriage Drive, Kensington Gdns SW7 🚇High St Kensington, South Kensington 🌐royalparks.org.uk

This grand Gothic Revival memorial to Prince Albert, Queen Victoria's beloved consort, was completed in 1872, 11 years after his death. Fittingly, it is near the site of the 1851 Exhibition, which Albert co-organized. The

←

The soaring interior of the Brompton Oratory, rich in Italianate decoration

statue, by John Foley, shows him with an exhibition catalogue on his knee.

The Queen chose Sir George Gilbert Scott to design the monument, which stands 55 m (175 ft) high. It is loosely based on a medieval market cross – although more elaborate, with a black and gilded spire, multi-coloured marble canopy, stones, mosaics, enamels, wrought iron and nearly 200 sculpted figures.

Having turned black over the years from pollution, the statue underwent a four-year renovation, and was unveiled in 1998 by Queen Elizabeth II.

Royal Albert Hall

📍C7 🚇Kensington Gore SW7 🚇High St Kensington, South Kensington ⏰For tours & performances daily 🌐royalalberthall.com

Completed in 1871, this huge concert hall was modelled on Roman amphitheatres.

On the elegant red-brick exterior the only ostentation is a frieze symbolizing the triumph of arts and science. Originally planned as the Hall of Arts and Science, Queen Victoria renamed i t in memory of her husband when she laid the foundation stone in 1868.

The hall is often used for classical concerts, such as the "Proms", but it also hosts other large events, like rock concerts and comedy shows. In preparation for its 150th anniversary in 2021, the hall is undergoing renovation, with a two-storey basement under excavation, but remains open.

Kensington Palace

📍B6 🚇Kensington Palace Gardens W8 🚇High St Kensington, Queensway, Notting Hill Gate ⏰Mar–Oct: 10am–6pm daily; Nov–Feb: 10am–4pm daily (last adm: 1 hr before closing) 🌐hrp.org.uk

Half of this spacious palace is used as royal apartments; the other half, which includes the 18th-century state rooms, is open to the public. When William of Orange and his wife Mary came to the throne in 1689, they bought a mansion, dating from 1605, and commissioned Christopher Wren to convert it into a royal palace.

The palace has seen some important royal events. In 1714, Queen Anne died here from apoplexy brought on by overeating and, on 20 June 1837, Princess Victoria of Kent was woken at 5am to be told that her uncle William IV had died and she was now queen – the start of her 64-year reign. After the death in 1997 of Diana, Princess of Wales, the gold gates to the south were deluged with bouquets in their thousands.

Visitors can explore inside the King's and Queen's state apartments, the latter little changed since it was designed for Mary in the 17th century. The palace also often displays clothes worn by many of the royals, including the Queen and Princess Diana.

→

The magnificent Royal Albert Hall in South Kensington

The Diana, Princess of Wales Memorial Playground

📍B6 🚇Kensington Gardens 🚌Bayswater, Queensway 🕐Daily, from 10am; closing times vary, from 4:45pm in midwinter to 7:45pm in midsummer 🌐royal parks.org.uk

The newest of Kensington Gardens' three playgrounds, on the site of an earlier playground funded by J M Barrie, takes the boy who didn't want to grow up as its theme and includes a beach cove with a 15-m (50-ft) pirates' galleon, a treehouse and a mermaid's fountain with a slumbering crocodile. Though all children under 13 must be accompanied by an adult, staff are on hand too. Many features of the playground are accessible to children with specific needs.

Kensington Gardens

📍C6 🚇W8 🚌Bayswater, High St Kensington, Queensway, Lancaster Gate 🕐6am–dusk daily 🌐royalparks.org.uk

The former grounds of Kensington Palace became a public park in 1841. The gardens are full of charm, starting with Sir George Frampton's statue (1912) of J M Barrie's fictional Peter Pan, playing his pipes for the bronze fairies and animals that cling to the column below. Just north of here are many lovely ornamental fountains and statues, while to the south is George Frederick Watts' muscular horse and rider, *Physical Energy*.

Close by is a summer house designed by William Kent in 1735. The Round Pond, built in 1728, is often packed with model boats navigated by enthusiasts young and old.

In the north, near Lancaster Gate, is a dogs' cemetery, created in 1880 by the then Duke of Cambridge.

Marble Arch

📍E5 🚇Park Lane W1 🚌Marble Arch

John Nash designed the arch in 1827 as the main entrance to Buckingham Palace. It was, however, too narrow for the grandest coaches and in 1851 it was moved here.

Historically, only senior members of the royal family and one of the royal artillery regiments are allowed to pass under it.

The arch stands near the site of the old Tyburn gallows, where until 1783 the city's most notorious criminals were hanged in front of crowds of blood-thirsty spectators.

Royal College of Art

📍C7 🚇Kensington Gore SW7 🚌High St Kensington, South Kensington 🕐For exhibitions, lectures, film screenings 🌐rca.ac.uk

Sir Hugh Casson's mainly glass-fronted building (1962) is in stark contrast to the Victoriana around it. The college was founded in 1837 to teach design and practical art for the manufacturing industries. It became noted for modern art in the 1950s and 1960s, when David Hockney, Peter Blake and Eduardo Paolozzi attended.

→

Passing the time aboard a rowing boat on Hyde Park's Serpentine

Hyde Park

📍 E6 🚇 W2 🚉 Hyde Park Corner, Knightsbridge, Lancaster Gate, Marble Arch ⏰ 5am–midnight daily 🌐 royalparks.org.uk

The ancient manor of Hyde was part of the lands of Westminster Abbey seized by Henry VIII on the Dissolution of the Monasteries in 1536. It has remained a royal park ever since. Henry used it for hunting, but James I opened it to the public in the early 17th century. The Serpentine, an artificial lake used for boating and bathing, was created when Caroline, George II's queen, dammed the flow of the Westbourne River in 1730. The Princess Diana Memorial Fountain is to the south of the Serpentine. In its time, the park has been a venue for

INSIDER TIP
On the Water

Rent a pedalo or rowing boat from the Boathouse (Apr–Oct) and enjoy a tranquil tour of Hyde Park's Serpentine lake. The brave can dive in for a swim at the lido during the summer months (Jun–early Sep).

duelling, horse racing, demonstrations and musical performances. The 1851 Great Exhibition was held here in a vast glass palace. Come Christmas time, the festive Winter Wonderland takes over, with markets, an ice rink and a funfair.

Speakers' Corner

📍 E5 🚇 Hyde Park W2 🚉 Marble Arch

An 1872 law made it legal for anyone to assemble an audience and address them on whatever topic they chose. Since then, this corner of Hyde Park has become the established venue for budding public orators and a fair number of eccentrics.

On Sunday mornings, speakers from fringe groups and one-member political parties reveal their plans for the betterment of humanity (or otherwise) while assembled onlookers heckle them.

KENSINGTON, HOLLAND PARK AND NOTTING HILL

From well-to-do High Street Kensington, the neighbourhoods to the north drift uphill through expensive townhouses, some original little museums and Holland Park. Partially wooded and beautifully landscaped, the park reflects its upmarket location with its pricey restaurants and outdoor operas. To its north is Notting Hill, more touristy than High Street Kensington, in part because of the eponymous film, but also because of its market on Portobello Road.

Brightly painted shops and houses ↓ on Portobello Road

DESIGN MUSEUM

📍 A7 🏠 224-8 Kensington High St W8 🚇 Kensington High St, Holland Park 🕐 10am-6pm daily (last entry 5pm) and till 8pm on first Fri of every month (last entry 7pm) 🌐 designmuseum.org

The Design Museum, housed in a truly unique building, is dedicated to every element of contemporary design, including architecture, transport, graphics, furniture and fashion. Its imaginatively curated temporary exhibitions usually outshine its rather small but nevertheless engaging permanent display.

GALLERY GUIDE

The permanent exhibition, called Designer Maker User, examines some of the most iconic product designs of the modern world. It also shows a cross-section of recent innovations from the three perspectives of its title.

Appropriately housed in what was the Commonwealth Institute, an inventively designed 1960s building, the Design Museum reopened in 2016, having moved from its previous riverside location near Tower Bridge. The building itself is a joy to behold, with its arresting interior of sweeping spaces and geometric lines all crowned by a dramatically cascading roof. Famed for this copper-plated hyperbolic parabol, the exterior was kept intact, but the interior completely re-fashioned. There is room enough for four galleries – three of them for the superlative programme of temporary exhibitions and one to house the excellent and occasionally interactive permanent collection, called Designer Maker User, which is free to explore.

The building also houses a lecture theatre, café and two appealing shops. The green woodland of Holland Park is right next door.

SHOP

Designer Shopping

The Design Museum shop is one of the best museum shops in London for the originality and diversity of its carefully selected stock. Items include clothing, stylish stationery, models and miniatures, prints, kitchenware and more.

↑ Attractive displays of innovative design feature in the permanent collection

EXPERIENCE MORE

Holland Park

A7 **Ilchester Place, W8** **Holland Park, High Street Kensington, Notting Hill Gate** **7:30am–dusk daily (hours vary with season)** **rbkc.gov.uk**

This small but delightful park, more wooded and intimate than the large royal parks to its east, Hyde Park and Kensington Gardens, was opened in 1952 on what remained of the grounds of the Jacobean Holland House – the rest had been sold off in the late 19th century for the construction of new, large houses. During its heyday in the 19th century, the mansion was a noted centre of social and political intrigue. Statesmen such as Charles James Fox mixed here with the likes of the poet Lord Byron, who met Lady Caroline Lamb here. The house suffered heavy bomb damage during World War II, but surviving parts and outbuildings have been put to various uses: exhibitions are held in the orangery and the ice house, and the old Garden Ballroom is now a restaurant. The former front terrace of the house is often used as a backdrop for summer musical events and open-air film screenings, and theatre, opera and dance performances.

The park still contains some of the formal gardens laid out in the early 19th century. Surprisingly, there is also a Japanese garden, created for the 1991 London Festival of Japan. Look out for koi carp in the pond beneath the waterfall. Colourful peacocks roam the grounds here, and there is a well-equipped playground perfect for kids to while away an afternoon in.

Museum of Brands, Packaging and Advertising

A4 **111-117 Lancaster Rd W11** **Ladbroke Grove** **10am–6pm Tue-Sat, 11am–5pm Sun** **museumofbrands.com**

This out-of-the-ordinary museum is at once a permanent exhibition for the history of product packaging in the UK, a study of the changing tastes and fashions since the Victorian period and a gleeful trip down memory lane. The sheer volume of items on display is dizzying: tins, bottles, boxes, magazines, toys, games, household appliances and much more besides. In the main exhibition space, the twisty Time Tunnel, familiar products appear multiple times, their packaging updated as the years pass. Other displays reflect past trends, like the Egyptomania of the 1920s and the militarization of marketing during the two World Wars. There's a section for every decade of the 20th and 21st centuries and some substantial and intriguing 19th-century displays,

← Stylized Japanese elegance in the Kyoto Garden, Holland Park

↑ Exquisite tilework in Eastern style in Leighton House's Arab Hall

such as the teapots, gift sets and guides from the Great Exhibition of 1851.

Leighton House
📍A7 🏠12 Holland Park Rd W14 🚇High St Kensington 🕐10am-5:30pm Wed-Mon 🌐rbkc.gov.uk/subsites/museums.aspx

Lord Leighton was one of the most respected Victorian painters. His work *Flaming June* is regarded by many as the apotheosis of the Pre-Raphaelite movement. His house, built in 1864-9, has been preserved with its opulent decoration as an extraordinary monument to the Victorian aesthetics Leighton embodied. The highlight is the Arab Hall, added in 1879 to house Leighton's collection of Islamic tiles, some inscribed with text from the Koran. There are paintings and drawings displayed, including some by Edward Burne-Jones, John Millais, G F Watts and many works by Leighton himself. There are free guided tours at 3pm on Wednesday and Sunday. Semi-regular "Leighton Lates", usually held once a month on a Friday, give visitors the chance to enjoy the house until 9pm, with complimentary live music and a glass of wine.

Notting Hill
📍A6 🏠W11 🚇Notting Hill Gate

Now the home of Europe's biggest street carnival, most of this area was farmland until the 19th century. In the 1950s and 60s, it became a centre for the Caribbean community, many of whom lived here when they first arrived in Britain. The riotous carnival started in 1966 and takes over the area every August bank holiday weekend, when costumed parades meander through the streets.

Kensington Square
📍B7 🏠W8 🚇High St Kensington

This is one of London's oldest squares. It was laid out in the 1680s, and a few early 18th-century houses still remain (Nos 11 and 12 are the oldest). The renowned philosopher John Stuart Mill lived at No 18, and the Pre-Raphaelite painter and illustrator Edward Burne-Jones at No 41.

Portobello Road
📍A5 🏠W11 🚇Notting Hill Gate, Ladbroke Grove 🕐Main market: 9am-7pm Fri & Sat; general market, bric-a-brac: 9am-6pm Mon-Wed & 9am-1pm Thu 🌐portobelloroad.co.uk

There has been a market here since 1837. Today the southern end of the road consists mostly of stalls that sell antiques, jewellery, souvenirs and other collectables. The market is extremely popular and tends to be very crowded, but it is well worth visiting, if only to experience its bustling, cheerful atmosphere. The busiest day is Saturday, when the antiques arcades are open. If you are looking for bargains, be warned – the stallholders have a sound idea of the value of what they are selling. Other markets run along the rest of the street on different days, with vintage and new clothes featured around Portobello Green, under Westway near Ladbroke Grove Tube (Fri–Sun).

REGENT'S PARK
AND MARYLEBONE

The residents of Marylebone are generally less aristocratic than their Mayfair counterparts, but this is still a genteel area with one of London's more high-brow high streets. There is a distinct change in tone on the main road between here and Regent's Park to the north, where the massive queues for Madame Tussauds are accompanied by non-stop traffic. This all melts pleasantly away in the attractive park itself, with its canalside location providing universal appeal.

↓ Marylebone High Street at dusk

↑ Entrance to the ever
popular London Zoo

→

Enjoying the underwater
view of penguins swimming
at Penguin Beach

LONDON ZOO

📍 F1 🏠 Regent's Park NW1 🚇 Camden Town, Regent's Park ⏰ Apr–Aug: 10am–6pm; Sep–Oct & Mar: 10am–5:30pm; Nov–Feb: 10am–4pm (last adm 1 hr before closing); times vary, check website 🌐 zsl.org

By international standards, London Zoo is relatively small but it packs a lot in, including Sumatran tigers, Western lowland gorillas, spider monkeys, giraffes, iguanas, pythons and bird-eating tarantulas.

Did You Know?

The zoo has more than 650 species and over 1,000 mammals, amphibians, birds and reptiles.

Despite its dense population, many of the larger animals here enjoy relatively spacious and interesting enclosures, especially since the zoo embarked on an extensive series of imaginative redevelopments in the early 2000s. Since then they have opened Penguin Beach, Gorilla Kingdom, Rainforest Life, the Meet the Monkeys and In with the Lemurs walk-through exhibits, with the Snowdon Aviary set to become a colobus monkey walk-through following a Foster + Partners reboot in 2020. The largest enclosure is the Land of the Lions, where Asiatic lions prowl around the zoo's rendering of the Gir Forest in western India. Visitors look on from walkways and an imagining of a Gujarat village, complete with train station, high street and temple ruins.

EXPERIENCE MORE

Wigmore Hall

Q G4 **⌂** 36 Wigmore St W1 **Ⓢ** Bond St, Oxford Circus **W** wigmore-hall. org.uk

This appealing little concert hall for chamber music was designed by T E Collcutt, architect of the Savoy hotel, in 1900. At first it was called Bechstein Hall because it was attached to the Bechstein piano show-room; the area used to be the heart of London's piano trade. Opposite is the Art Nouveau emporium built in 1907 as Debenham and Freebody's department store – now known as Debenhams.

Madame Tussauds

Q F3 **⌂** Marylebone Rd NW1 **Ⓢ** Baker St **⊙** 9am-4pm Mon-Fri, 9am-5pm Sat & Sun; hours vary, check website **W** madame tussauds.com

Madame Tussaud began her wax-modelling career rather morbidly, making death masks of well-known victims of the French Revolution. In 1835 she set up an exhibition of her work in Baker Street, not far from the present site.

Traditional wax-modelling techniques are still used to recreate politicians, royals, actors, rock stars and sporting heroes, the displays changing fairly regularly to keep up with who's in and who's out.

The exhibition features "Party", where visitors can "attend" a celebrity bash; "Film", devoted to Hollywood's finest, such as Marilyn Monroe and ET; and "Royals", where you can step onto the palace balcony with Her Majesty. "Culture" has the likes of Shakespeare and Picasso, and the "Music Zone" includes Ed Sheeran, Rihanna and Lady Gaga. There are also sections dedicated to franchises such as Marvel and Star Wars, with detailed walk-in sets and a 4D Marvel film experience. "Sherlock Holmes Experience" has a theatrical sense of Victorian melodrama, and in "Spirit of London" visitors travel in stylized London taxi-cabs through momentous events in the city's history, from the Great Fire of 1666 to 1960s Swinging London.

Ticket prices are fairly steep, but cheaper if you buy online in advance. Opting for timed tickets can help reduce queuing times.

Lord's Cricket Ground

Q D2 **⌂** NW8 **Ⓢ** St John's Wood **⊙** For guided tours: Jan- Feb 11am-2pm; Apr-Oct 10am-3pm; Mar, Nov & Dec 10am-2pm **⏰** Last 10 days of Dec **W** lords.org

Set up in 1814 by professional cricketer Thomas Lord, the ground can be visited on guided tours that take in the Long Room, the dressing rooms and the Marylebone Cricket Club Museum. This is full of memorabilia from cricketing history, including a stuffed sparrow killed by a cricket ball and the Ashes. This tiny

→ The late-Victorian pavilion at Lord's Cricket Ground

urn contains, supposedly, the burned remains of a cricket bail signifying "the death of English cricket" after a notable defeat by Australia. It is still the object of ferocious competition between the two national teams. The museum explains the history of the game, and mementos of notable cricketers make it a place of pilgrimage for devotees of the sport. Tours are hourly and it is essential to book ahead; there are no tours on major match days, but ticket holders do get free access to the museum.

Broadcasting House

📍 G4 🏠 Portland Place W1 🚇 Oxford Circus 🌐 bbc.co.uk

Broadcasting House was built in 1931 as a suitably modern Art Deco setting for the new medium of broadcasting. Its front, curving with the street, is dominated by Eric Gill's stylized relief *Prospero and Ariel*, inspired by characters in Shakespeare's play *The Tempest*. As the invisible spirit of the air, Ariel was considered an appropriate personification of broadcasting. The character appears in two other sculptures on the western frontage, and again over the eastern entrance in the frieze *Ariel Piping to Children*. Broadcasting

House is the London headquarters of BBC news, radio, television and online departments. The only way to get a look inside is to book yourself a place, via the website, on one of the BBC's television or radio shows as a studio audience member.

A new wing added in 2005 was named after the disc jockey John Peel. Further refurbishment in 2011 created a public piazza, a BBC shop and a café that overlooks the central newsroom.

Oxford Street

📍 F5 🏠 W1 🚇 Marble Arch, Bond St, Oxford Circus, Tottenham Court Rd 🌐 oxfordstreet.co.uk

This is London's biggest and busiest shopping street, running from Marble Arch at the western end right along Marylebone's southern border and then beyond, dividing Soho and Fitzrovia and ending at the Centre Point tower block. The western half of the street is home to several department stores, most notably Selfridges, the largest and most famous (don't miss its magnificent Food Hall), although John Lewis, opened in 1864, predates it by half a century. Along the street's length and its shopper-clogged pavements are the UK flagship stores

of brands such as Nike, UNIQLO and Gap plus British favourites like Marks & Spencer and Topshop.

Sherlock Holmes Museum

📍 E3 🏠 221b Baker St NW1 🚇 Baker St 🕐 9:30am–6pm daily 🌐 sherlock-holmes. co.uk

Sir Arthur Conan Doyle's fictional detective lived at 221b Baker Street, an address that did not exist at the time, because Baker Street was then much shorter. This building, dating from 1815, is on what Conan Doyle would have known as Upper Baker Street, above Marylebone Road. It has been converted to resemble Holmes's flat, and is furnished exactly as described in the books. Visitors are greeted by Holmes's "housekeeper" and shown to his recreated rooms on the first floor. The shop sells souvenirs including short stories and deerstalker hats.

Did You Know?

There have been more films starring Sherlock Holmes than any other (human) character.

HAMPSTEAD AND HIGHGATE

Separated by the rolling fields and woodlands of Hampstead Heath and the atmospheric Highgate Cemetery, two of the biggest draws for visitors, the "villages" of Hampstead and Highgate have maintained much of their quaintness and independence, despite London's rapid urban expansion. The jumbled streets graced with boutique shops and upmarket restaurants that make up the old villages are great for a stroll in a part of the city where the pace is noticeably slower.

Cycling through
↓ the woodland on
Hampstead Heath

↑ View over London from the green
   environs of Hampstead Heath

HAMPSTEAD HEATH

📍C1 🏠Hampstead NW3, NW5 🚇Belsize Park, Hampstead, Kentish Town, Golders
Green 🚆Hampstead Heath, Gospel Oak 🕐24 hrs daily 🌐Hampstead Heath:
cityoflondon.gov.uk; Kenwood House: english-heritage.org.uk

**A favourite green space among Londoners, Hampstead Heath is the largest
of inner London's parklands, though it is too wild and wonderfully unkept
to be considered a proper park.**

The sprawling heath, separating the hilltop
villages of Hampstead and Highgate, brings
a slice of the countryside to the city, with
large tracts of wild woodlands and meadows
rolling over hills and around ponds and lakes.
Covering an area of 8 sq km (3 sq miles), its
natural habitats attract a wealth of wildlife,
including bats and some 180 species of
birds. There are also all kinds of landscaped
areas, most notably the Hill Garden, a
charming Edwardian garden once the
grounds to Lord Leverhulme's house, but
now its raised pergola walkway, flowering
plants and beautiful formal pond are open
to all. Among the many other features of
the heath are Vale of Health, an isolated
village tucked inside the southern boundary,
and the picturesque Viaduct Pond.

HIGHGATE CEMETERY

📍G1 🏠Swain's Lane N6 🚇Archway 🕐Check website for
opening hours 🌐highgatecemetery.org

Opened in 1839, this is London's best-known cemetery,
most famous for epitomizing the Victorian obsession
with death and the afterlife.

EXPERIENCE Hampstead and Highgate

The two leafy sections of Highgate Cemetery, divided by
a country lane, are full of flowerbeds, statues, elaborate
tombs and overgrown gravestones, bathed in a light
suitably subdued by the shade from the small forests of
trees. For Victorians, preoccupied with death and insistent
on burial rather than cremation, this was the graveyard
of choice, where you could lie shoulder to shoulder with
poets, artists and intellectuals. Both sections contain
the graves of numerous iconic figures but it is the West
Cemetery which is the more atmospheric, and architec-
turally interesting. Its showpiece is the restored Egyptian
Avenue, a street of family vaults styled on ancient
Egyptian tombs, leading to the Circle of Lebanon,
a ring of vaults topped by a cedar tree.

Statue of an angel, one
of many found among
the tombs and trees ↑

↑ Karl Marx's tomb in its
tranquil surroundings
in Highgate Cemetery

EXPERIENCE MORE

Freud Museum

📍C1 🏠20 Maresfield
Gdns NW3 🚇Finchley Rd
🕐Noon–5pm Wed–Sun
📅1 Jan, 25–26 Dec
🌐freud.org.uk

In 1938, Sigmund Freud, the founder of psychoanalysis, fled from Nazi persecution in Vienna to this Hampstead house. Making use of the possessions he brought with him, his family recreated the atmosphere of his Vienna consulting rooms.

After Freud died in 1939 his daughter Anna (who was a pioneer of child psychoanalysis) kept the house as it was, and in 1986 it was opened as a museum dedicated to her father. On display is the couch on which patients lay for analysis. A series of 1930s home movies shows Freud with his dog as well as more distressing footage of Nazi attacks on his apartment. There's a bookshop and free tours or talks take place at 2pm on Wednesdays. In 2016 Anna Freud was commemorated with her own blue plaque on the house, joining that of her father, the 19th-century building in London to have been awarded the rare "double blue" accolade. Other properties with two blue plaques include 29 Fitzroy Square and the Handel and Hendrix house.

Keats House

📍C1 🏠10 Keats Grove
NW3 🚇Hampstead,
Belsize Park 🚉Hampstead
Heath 🕐11am–5pm Wed–
Sun 📅Christmas week
🌐cityoflondon.gov.
uk/keats

Originally two semi-detached houses built in 1816, the smaller one became Keats's home in 1818, when a friend persuaded him to move in. Keats spent two productive years here: perhaps his most celebrated poem *Ode to a Nightingale* was said to have been written under a plum tree in the garden. The Brawne family moved into the larger house a year later and Keats became engaged

to their daughter, Fanny. However, the marriage never took place: Keats died of consumption in Rome before two years had passed. He was only 25 years old. A copy of one of Keats's love letters to Fanny, the engagement ring he offered her and a lock of her hair are among the mementos exhibited at the house, whose displays were revamped for its 200th anniversary in 2018. Visitors are also able to see copies of some of Keats's manuscripts, part of a collection that serves as a tribute to his life and work. Thirty-minute tours begin at 1:30pm and 3pm.

Burgh House

📍C1 🏠New End Sq NW3
🚇Hampstead 🕐Noon–
5pm Wed–Fri & Sun 📅3
weeks at Christmas
🌐burghhouse.org.uk

Since 1979, an independent trust has run Burgh House as the Hampstead Museum, which illustrates the history of the area and some of its notable residents. The museum owns a significant art collection, including a work by the Bloomsbury Group painter Duncan Grant, along with furniture and archive material on the area. There is a display about Hampstead as a spa in the 18th and 19th centuries. In the 1720s, Dr William Gibbons, chief physician to the spa, lived at this address.

DRINK

The Spaniards Inn

Dickensian pub on Hampstead Heath with a colourful 500-year history, a beer garden for summer and an open fire in winter.

📍C1 🏠Spaniards Rd
NW3 🌐thespaniards
hampstead.co.uk

GREENWICH AND CANARY WHARF

Separated by the river, but joined by a foot tunnel underneath it, Greenwich and Canary Wharf are as different from one another as it gets. Built around the old docks in the 1980s, the business district of Canary Wharf lacks soul but is full of hidden history and dockside walk-ing routes, the sum of which makes it unlike anywhere else in the city. In contrast, Greenwich has history seeping from its pores, populated as it is by a swathe of prominent royal and historical build-ings and museums, an ancient park and a handsome town centre.

Looking over maritime Greenwich and towards Canary Wharf ↓

EXPERIENCE

Old Royal Naval College

📍 N9 🏠 King William Walk SE10 🚇 Cutty Sark DLR, Greenwich DLR 🚂 Greenwich, Maze Hill 🕐 10am–5pm daily; grounds: 8am–11pm daily 🚫 24–26 Dec & some Sat 🌐 ornc.org

A landmark of Greenwich, these ambitious buildings by Christopher Wren were built on the site of the old 15th-century royal palace, where Tudors Henry VIII, Mary I and Elizabeth I were born, to house naval pensioners. At its peak, the then hospital was home to some 2,700 veterans. The Painted Hall, which was intended as a dining room for the retired seamen, was opulently decorated by Sir James Thornhill in the early 18th century. The tremendous ceiling mural is the largest figurative painting in the country. In 1805, the hall was the location of a lavish lying-in-state ceremony for Lord Horatio Nelson, who was killed at the Battle of Trafalgar.

The hall reopened in 2019 following an extensive conservation and cleaning project, with a new entrance via the vaulted King William Undercroft – itself restored to something close to its original Baroque splendour. Ceiling tours, which need to be booked in advance, climb to the top of an observation deck to view the painting's detail at close hand. There are also free guided walking tours of the site several times a day, for which no booking is required. They start from the visitor centre and last about 45 minutes.

In 1873, the hospital was acquired by the Naval College in Portsmouth and remained a training post for officers until 1997. It also trained thousands of Wrens during World War II. There is a relaxed pub next to the visitor centre with a terrace overlooking the *Cutty Sark*, but visitors are also welcome to picnic in the grounds – provided that they dispose of litter thoughtfully.

Royal Observatory

📍 O10 🏠 Greenwich Park SE10 🚇 Cutty Sark DLR 🚂 Greenwich 🕐 10am–5pm daily (to 6pm Easter & Jun–Sep) 🚫 24–26 Dec 🌐 rmg.co.uk

The meridian (0° longitude) that divides Earth's eastern and western hemispheres passes through here, and millions of visitors come to be photographed standing with a foot on either side of it. In 1884, Greenwich Mean Time became the basis of time measurement for most

↑ The onion dome of the Royal Observatory Greenwich, housing a colossal telescope

of the world. Here you can journey through the history of time, explore how scientists first began to map the stars and see world-changing inventions, including the UK's largest refracting telescope. Visitors can even touch a 4.5-billion-year-old asteroid. The stately original building, Flamsteed House, was designed by Christopher Wren for the first Astronomer Royal, John Flamsteed. It contains original instruments belonging to his successors, including Edmond Halley, as well as the celebrated sea clocks of John Harrison, including the H4 – arguably the most important timepiece ever made. There is also a state-of-the-art planetarium here, the only one in London. There is an entry charge for Flamsteed House and the planetarium shows; the Astronomy Centre is free.

The structure holding the copper hull of the impressive *Cutty Sark* ↑

Canary Wharf

📍N8 🏠E14 🚇Canary Wharf, West India Quay DLR

London's most ambitious commercial development opened in 1991, when the first tenants moved into the 50-storey One Canada Square. At 235 m (700 ft), it continues to dominate the city's eastern skyline with its pyramid-shaped top. The tower stands on what was the West India Dock, closed, like all the London docks, between the 1960s and the 1980s, when trade moved to Tilbury. Today, Canary Wharf is thriving, with a major shopping complex, cafés and restaurants.

Emirates Air Line

📍O8 🏠Western Gateway E16/Edmund Halley Way SE10 🚇Royal Victoria DLR, North Greenwich 🕐7am-11pm Mon-Fri, 8am-11pm Sat, 9am-11pm Sun (to 9pm Sun-Thu Oct-Mar) 🌐emiratesairline.co.uk

This cable car, crossing the Thames between the Royal Victoria Dock and the O2, provides spectacular views during the five-minute trip. It's a magnificent way to cross the river. Travelcards or Oyster Pay as you go provide a 25 per cent discount. In the evenings the "flights" slow down, giving you more time to enjoy the panorama of city lights.

Cutty Sark

📍N9 🏠King William Walk SE10 🚇Cutty Sark DLR 🚢Greenwich Pier 🕐10am-5pm daily (last adm: 4:15pm) 🕐24-26 Dec 🌐rmg.co.uk

This majestic vessel is a survivor of the clippers that crossed the Atlantic and Pacific oceans in the 19th century. Launched in 1869 as a tea carrier, it was something of a speed machine in its day, returning from Australia in 1884 in just 83 days – 25 days faster than any other ship. It made its final voyage in 1938 and was put on display here in 1957. In 2006 the *Cutty Sark* was closed to visitors for renovation work, which suffered a major setback in May 2007 when the ship was severely damaged by fire. It was reopened by the Queen in spring 2012, fully restored and slightly raised in a glass enclosure. Visitors can explore the cargo decks and sleeping quarters below deck, take the ship's wheel, and be entertained by tales from the costumed "crew". There are interactive displays on navigation and life on board.

Greenwich Park

📍 O10 🏠 SE10 🚇 Cutty Sark DLR, Greenwich DLR 🚉 Greenwich, Maze Hill, Blackheath ⏰ 6am–6pm or dusk 🌐 royalparks. org.uk

Originally the grounds of a royal palace and still a Royal Park, Greenwich Park was enclosed in 1433 and its brick wall built in the reign of James I. Later, in the 17th century, the French royal landscape gardener André Le Nôtre was invited to redesign the park. The broad avenue, rising south up the hill, was part of his plan. It's a steep climb up the hilltop but one well-rewarded by sweeping views across

London and more green space to explore.

Greenwich Foot Tunnel

📍 N9 🏠 Between Greenwich Pier SE10 and Isle of Dogs E14 🚇 Island Gardens, Cutty Sark DLR 🚉 Greenwich Pier ⏰ 24hrs daily

This 370-m- (1,200-ft-) long tunnel was opened in 1902 to allow south London labourers to walk to work in Millwall Docks. It is well worth making the crossing from Greenwich for the wonderful views, once above ground, back across the river, of Christopher Wren's Royal Naval College and of Inigo Jones's Queen's House.

Matching round red-brick terminals, with glass domes, mark the top of the lift shafts on either side of the river. Both ends of the tunnel are close to stations on the Docklands Light Railway (DLR). Although there are security cameras, the tunnel can be eerie at night.

The Fan Museum

📍 N10 🏠 12 Croom's Hill SE10 🚉 Greenwich ⏰ 11am–5pm Tue–Sat, noon–5pm Sun 🚫 1 Jan, 24–26 Dec 🌐 thefan museum.org.uk

One of London's most unusual museums owes

its existence and appeal to the enthusiasm of Helene Alexander, whose personal collection of about 4,000 fans from the 17th century onwards has been augmented by donations. A small permanent exhibition looks at types of fans and fanmaking, while the collection is rotated in temporary displays. On some days, afternoon tea is served in the orangery.

The O2 Arena

📍 O8 🏠 North Greenwich SE10 🚇 North Greenwich ⏰ 9am–late 🌐 theo2. co.uk

The former Millennium Dome was the focal point of Britain's celebration of the year 2000. Controversial from its earliest days, it is nonetheless an amazing feat of engineering. Its canopy is made from 100,000 sq m (109,000 sq yards) of Teflon-coated spun glass-fibre, and is supported by over 70 km (43 miles) of steel cable rigged to a dozen 100-m (328-ft) masts. Now London's largest indoor concert venue, the O2 also has bars, restaurants, a cinema and IndigO2, a smaller venue. You can also don climbing gear and ascend the outside along a long, bouncy walkway to the very top.

BEFORE YOU GO

Forward planning is essential to any successful trip. Be prepared for all eventualities by considering the following points before you travel.

AT A GLANCE

CURRENCY
Pound Sterling (GBP)

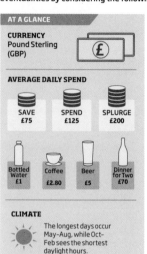

AVERAGE DAILY SPEND

SAVE	SPEND	SPLURGE
£75	£125	£200

Bottled Water	Coffee	Beer	Dinner for Two
£1	£2.80	£5	£70

CLIMATE

The longest days occur May–Aug, while Oct–Feb sees the shortest daylight hours.

Temperatures average 22°C (75°F) in summer. Winter can be very cold and icy.

The heaviest rainfall is in October and November, but showers occur all year round.

ELECTRICITY SUPPLY

Power sockets are type G, fitting three-pronged plugs. Standard voltage is 230 volts.

Passports and Visas

For a stay of up to six months for the purpose of tourism, citizens of the US, Canada, Australia and New Zealand do not need a visa to enter the country. New arrangements for EU citizens, currently able to settle permanently, are likely to be put in place after the UK leaves the EU. Consult your nearest British embassy or check the **UK Government** website for up-to-date visa information specific to your home country.
UK Government 🅦 gov.uk/check-uk-visa

Travel Safety Advice

Visitors can get up-to-date travel safety information from the UK Foreign and Commonwealth Office, the US State Department, and the Department of Foreign Affairs and Trade in Australia.
Australia 🅦 smartraveller.gov.au
UK 🅦 gov.uk/foreign-travel-advice
US 🅦 travel.state.gov

Customs Information

An individual is permitted to carry the following within the EU for personal use:

  Tobacco products: 800 cigarettes, 400 cigarillos, 200 cigars or 1 kg of smoking tobacco.

  Alcohol: 10 litres of spirits, 20 litres of fortified wines, 90 litres of wine and 110 litres of beer.

  Cash: If you plan to enter or leave the EU with €10,000 or more in cash (or the equivalent in other currencies) you must declare it to the customs authorities.

  These regulations may be subject to change once post-Brexit arrangements are put in place by the government, so consult the UK Government website for the most up-to-date customs information.

If travelling outside the EU limits vary so check restrictions before you set off.

Insurance

It is wise to take out an insurance policy covering theft, loss of belongings, medical problems, cancellation and delays.

Emergency treatment is usually free from the National Health Service, and there are reciprocal arrangements with other EEA countries, Australia, New Zealand and some others (check the **NHS** website for details).

Specialist care, drugs and repatriation are costly. Residents of EEA countries should carry a European Health Insurance Card (**EHIC**), which allows treatment for free or at a reduced cost. It is advisable for visitors from outside the EEA, Australia and New Zealand to arrange their own comprehensive medical insurance.

EHIC W gov.uk/european-health-insurance-card
NHS W nhs.uk

Vaccinations

No inoculations are needed for the UK.

Money

Major credit and debit cards are accepted in most shops and restaurants, while prepaid currency cards are accepted in some. Contactless payments are widely accepted in London, including on public transport. However, it is always worth carrying some cash, as many smaller businesses and markets still operate a cash-only policy. Cash machines are conveniently located at banks, train stations, shopping areas and main streets.

Booking Accommodation

London offers a huge variety of accommodation to suit any budget, including luxury five-star hotels, family-run B&Bs and budget hostels.

Lodgings can fill up and prices become inflated during during the summer, so it's worth booking well in advance.

A comprehensive list of accommodation to suit all needs can be found on **Visit London**, London's official tourist information website.

Visit London W visitlondon.com

Travellers with Specific Needs

Accessibility information for public transport is available from the TFL website.

In the City, Westminster, Camden and Kensington and Chelsea, a disabled driver badge allows you to park in blue-badge bays only.

The Visit London website offers handy tips on the city's accessibility provisions. **AccessAble** has a useful searchable online directory.

Museums and galleries offer audio tours, which are useful to those with impaired vision. **Action on Hearing Loss** and the **Royal National Institute for the Blind** can also offer useful information and advice.

AccessAble W accessable.org.uk
Action on Hearing Loss W actionhearingloss.org.uk
The Royal National Institute for the Blind W rnib.org.uk

Language

London is a multicultural city, in which you will hear many languages spoken. Many attractions and tour companies offer foreign language tours.

Closures

Mondays Some museums and tourist attractions are closed for the day.
Sundays Most shops close early or for the day.
Public holidays Schools and public services are closed for the day; some shops, museums and attractions either close early or for the day.

GETTING AROUND

London has one of the busiest public transport systems in Europe; understanding how it works will help you make the most of your trip.

AT A GLANCE

PUBLIC TRANSPORT COSTS

SINGLE BUS JOURNEY

£1.50

Zone 1-9
(flat fare)

SINGLE TUBE JOURNEY

£2.40

Zone 1-2
(off peak)

DAILY TRAVELCARD

£12.80

Zone 1-6
(off peak)

SPEED LIMIT

MOTORWAY

70 mph
(112 kmph)

DUAL CARRIAGEWAYS

70 mph
(112 kmph)

SINGLE CARRIAGEWAYS

60 mph
(96 kmph)

URBAN AREAS

30 mph
(48 kmph)

Arriving by Air

Five airports serve London: Heathrow, Gatwick, Stansted, Luton and London City. With the exception of London City Airport, all are situated a significant distance from central London, with good transport connections to the city centre. For the best rates, book tickets in advance.

Train Travel

International Train Travel

St Pancras International is the London terminus for Eurostar, the high-speed train linking the UK with the Continent. You can buy tickets and passes for multiple international journeys via **Eurail** or **Interrail**; advance reservations are usually not required but always check that your pass is valid on the service on which you wish to travel before attempting to board. **Eurostar** run a regular service from Paris, Brussels and Amsterdam to London via the Channel Tunnel. **Eurotunnel** operates a drive-on-drive-off train service between Calais and Folkestone.
Eurail W eurail.com; **Eurostar** W eurostar. com; **Eurotunnel** W eurotunnel.com; **Interrail** W interrail.eu

Domestic Train Travel

Lines are run by several different companies, but they are coordinated by **National Rail**, which operates a joint information service. London has eight main railway terminals serving different parts of Britain (Charing Cross, Euston, King's Cross, London Bridge, St Pancras, Paddington, Waterloo and Victoria). There are also over 300 smaller London stations. Each main terminus is the starting point for local and suburban lines that cover the whole of southeast England. London's local and suburban train lines are used by hundreds of thousands of commuters every

day. For visitors, rail services are most useful for trips to the outskirts of London and areas of the city without nearby Underground connections (especially in south London). If you are planning to travel outside of the capital, always try to book rail tickets in advance.
National Rail W nationalrail.co.uk

Long-Distance Bus Travel

Coaches from European and UK destinations arrive at Victoria Coach Station. The biggest operator in the UK is **National Express**. **Eurolines** is its European arm, offering coach routes to London from other European cities. Fares start from around £12 and vary depending on distance. Book in advance.
Eurolines W eurolines.eu
National Express W nationalexpress.com

Public Transport

Most public transport in London is coordinated by Transport for London (**TFL**), London's main public transport authority. Timetables, ticket information, transport maps and more can be found on their website.
TFL W tfl.gov.uk

Fare Zones
TFL divides the city into six charging zones for Underground, Overground and National Rail services, radiating out from Zone 1 in the centre. On buses, there is a flat fare for each trip, no matter how far you travel.

Tickets
Tube and rail fares are expensive, especially individual tickets. If you expect to make multiple trips around the city in a short space of time, you can buy a one-day off-peak Travelcard, which gives unlimited travel on all systems after 9:30am on weekdays (or any time on Saturday, Sunday and public holidays) within Zones 1–4 or 1–6 for a flat fee. If you wish to travel more freely, purchase a pay-as-you-go Oyster card or Visitor Oyster card (valid for all London zones), which you can preload and top up with credit (note

that a £5 deposit is required when buying an Oyster card and you will need one card per person). You can also use contactless credit or debit cards in the same way as the Oyster card. It is cheaper to pay as you go using contactless or Oyster as fares are subject to daily and weekly caps. When using public transport, you "touch in" with your card on a yellow card reader, and the corresponding amount is deducted. On Underground, DLR and Overground trains, you must also remember to "touch out" where you finish your journey, or you will be charged a maximum fare, though the excess can usually be reclaimed via the website if you forget. Prices are higher during peak times: 6:30–9:30am and 4–7pm Mon–Fri. Buy Travelcards and Oyster cards at Underground and local rail stations, or any shop that has the TFL "Ticket Stop" sticker in the window. You can also buy them from TFL before arriving; delivery is available to over 60 countries. Many smaller stations do not have staffed ticket counters, just self-service machines.

The Underground and DLR
The London Underground (commonly referred to as "the Tube") has 11 lines, all named and colour-coded, which intersect at various stations. The construction of an additional line, the Elizabeth line, is currently underway. Following setbacks, this will open in 2020 at the earliest. Some lines, like the Jubilee, have a single branch; others, like the Northern, have more than one, so it is important to check the digital boards on the platform and the destination on the front of the train. Trains run every few minutes 7:30–9:30am and 4–7pm, and every 5–10 minutes at all other times. The Central, Jubilee, Northern, Victoria and Piccadilly lines offer a 24-hour service on Fridays and Saturdays. All other lines operate 5am–12:40am Mon–Sat; reduced hours Sun. The DLR (Docklands Light Railway) is an overground network of trains that run from the City to stops in east and southeast London, including City Airport. Stations with disabled access are marked on Tube maps, which are located on all trains.

The Overground
Marked on Tube maps by an orange line, the Overground connects with the Underground and main railway stations at various points across the city. It operates in much the same way as the Underground, and covers most areas of the city without nearby Underground connections.

Bus
Slower but cheaper than the Tube, buses are also a good way of seeing the city as you travel. Bus routes are displayed on the TFL website and on maps at bus stops. The destination and route number is indicated on the front of the bus and the stops are announced on board. Buses do not accept cash so a ticket, Oyster card or contactless payment is required. A single fare costs £1.50, while unlimited bus travel caps out at £4.50 – just use the same card each time you use the bus to reach the daily cap.

The hopper fare allows you to make a second bus journey for free within an hour of travel. Travel is free on buses for under-16s as long as they carry a Zip Oyster card. Apply for one on the TFL website at least four weeks before you are due to arrive.

The Night buses (indicated by the letter "N" added before the route number) run on many popular routes from 11pm until 6am, generally 3–4 times per hour up to 2 or 3am. They cost slightly more than regular buses.

Taxis
London's iconic black cabs can be hailed on the street, booked online or over the phone, or picked up at taxi ranks throughout the city. The yellow "Taxi" sign is lit up when the taxi is free. The driver's cab licence number should be displayed in the back of the taxi. All taxis are metered, and fares start from £3. Taxi apps such as Uber also operate in London. The following services can be booked by phone or online:

Dial-a-Cab
ⓦ dialacab.co.uk
Gett Taxis
ⓦ gett.com/uk
Licensed London Taxi
ⓦ licensedlondontaxi.co.uk

Driving
EU driving licences issued by any of the EU member states are valid throughout the European Union. This situation may change following the UK's departure from the EU. If visiting from outside the EU, you may need to apply for an International Driving Permit. Check with your local automobile association before you travel, or consult the UK Driver and Vehicle Licensing Agency (**DVLA**).
DVLA
ⓦ gov.uk/driving-nongb-licence

Driving in London
Driving in London is not recommended. Traffic is slow moving, parking is scarce and expensive, and in central London there is the added cost of the **Congestion Charge** – an £11.50 daily charge for driving in central London 7am–6pm Mon–Fri.

In the event of an accident, contact the **AA** for roadside assistance.
AA
ⓦ theaa.com
Congestion Charge
ⓦ tfl.gov.uk/modes/driving/congestion-charge

Parking
Parking is prohibited at all times wherever the street is marked with double yellow or red lines by the kerb. If there is a single yellow line, parking is normally allowed from 6:30pm–8am Mon–Sat and all day Sun, but exact hours vary, so always check the signs along each street before leaving your vehicle. Where there is no line at all, parking is free at all times, but this is rare in central London. Rental car drivers are still liable for parking fines.

Car Rental

To rent a car in the UK you must be 21 or over (or in some cases, 25) and have held a valid driver's licence for at least a year.

Driving out of central London will take about an hour in any direction, more during rush hours; if you want to tour the countryside, it can be easier to take a train to a town or city outside London and rent a car from there.

Rules of the Road

Drive on the left. Seat belts must be worn at all times by the driver and all passengers. Children up to 135 cm tall or the age 12 or under must travel with the correct child restraint for their weight and size. Mobile telephones may not be used while driving except with a "hands-free" system, and third-party insurance is required by law. Overtake on the outside or right-hand lane, and when approaching a roundabout, give priority to traffic approaching from the right, unless indicated otherwise. All vehicles must give way to emergency services vehicles. It is illegal to drive in bus lanes during certain hours. See roadside signs for restrictions. The drink-drive limit is strictly enforced.

Cycling

You need a strong nerve to cycle in London's traffic, but it can be a great way to see the city. **Santander Cycles**, London's self-service cycle hire, has docking stations in central London. Bikes can also be rented from the **London Bicycle Tour Company** and other rental companies throughout the city. Be aware that drink-drive limits also apply to cyclists.

Santander Cycles
ⓦ tfl.gov.uk/modes/cycling/santander-cycles
London Bicycle Tour Company
ⓦ londonbicycle.com

Walking

Walking is a rewarding way to get around in London. The centre is not large, and you will be surprised at how short the distance is between places that seem far apart on the Tube.

Boats and Ferries

Car ferries from Calais and Dunkirk arrive in Dover, around 2 hours' drive from London.

Passenger and car-ferry services also sail from other ports in northern France to the south of England, as well as from Bilbao and Santander in Spain to Portsmouth or Plymouth. Ferry services also run to other ports around the country from the Netherlands and the Republic of Ireland.

London by Boat

Some of London's most spectacular views can be seen from the River Thames. **MBNA Thames Clippers** runs river services every 20 minutes on catamarans between Westminster or Battersea Power Station and North Greenwich in both directions, via the London Eye, Bankside and Tower Bridge, with some boats continuing east to Woolwich. The Tate Boat, or RB2, is also operated by MBNA Thames Clippers and runs between the Tate Britain and Tate Modern museums.

Standard tickets cost £8.40 in the central zone, but discounted fares apply if bought online or when using a Travelcard, contactless or Oyster. Discounted fares on the Tate Boat are also available if bought at either Tate or on Millbank or Bankside piers.

A number of providers offer river tours and experiences on the Thames, with numerous options available, from dining experiences to hop-on-hop-off services.

MBNA Thames Clippers
ⓦ thamesclippers.com
River Tours
ⓦ tfl.gov.uk/modes/river/about-river-tours

PRACTICAL INFORMATION

A little local know-how goes a long way in London. Here you will find all the essential advice and information you will need during your stay.

AT A GLANCE

EMERGENCY NUMBERS

GENERAL EMERGENCY

999

TIME ZONE
GMT/BST
British Summer
Time (BST) runs
end Mar–end Oct
EST -5; AEDT +11

TAP WATER
Tap water
in the UK is
safe to drink.

TIPPING

Waiter	10–12.5%
Hotel Porter	£1 per bag
Housekeeping	£1–2 per day
Concierge	£1–2
Taxi Driver	10%

Personal Security

Pickpockets work crowded tourist areas. Use your common sense and be alert to your surroundings. If you are unfortunate enough to have anything stolen, report the crime as soon as possible to the nearest police station. Get a copy of the crime report in order to claim on your insurance.

Contact your embassy if you have your passport stolen, or in the event of a serious crime or accident.

Health

For minor ailments go to a pharmacy or chemist. These are plentiful throughout the city; chains such as Boots and Superdrug have branches in almost every shopping district or in the city. If you have an accident or medical problem requiring non-urgent medical attention, you can find details of your nearest non-emergency medical service on the NHS website. Alternatively, you can call the NHS helpline number at any hour on 111, or go to your nearest Accident and Emergency (A&E) department. You may need a doctor's prescription to obtain certain pharmaceuticals; the pharmacist can inform you of the closest doctor's surgery or medical centre where you can be seen by a GP (general practitioner).

EU citizens can receive emergency medical treatment in the UK free of charge; however, this situation may change following the UK's departure from the EU.

Visitors from outside the EU may have to pay upfront for medical treatment and reclaim on insurance at a later date.

Smoking, Alcohol and Drugs

The UK has a smoking ban in all public places, including bars, cafés, restaurants, public transport, train stations and hotels. The UK legal limit for drivers is 80 mg of alcohol per 100 ml of blood, or 0.08 per cent BAC (blood alcohol content). This is roughly equivalent to one small glass of wine or a pint of regular-strength lager; however, it is best to avoid drinking altogether if you plan to drive. The possession of illegal drugs is prohibited and could result in a prison sentence.

ID

There is no requirement for visitors to carry ID, but in the case of a routine check you may be asked to show your passport and visa documentation. It is always useful to carry a photocopy of your passport ID page.

Local Customs

Always stand to the right on escalators or stairwells. Allow passengers to exit before you board public transport. On the Tube, it is customary to offer your seat to passengers who are less able-bodied, pregnant or elderly.

Visiting Churches and Cathedrals

Dress respectfully: cover your torso and upper arms. Ensure shorts and skirts cover your knees.

Mobile Phones and Wi-Fi

Free Wi-Fi hotspots are widely available in the city centre. Cafés and restaurants will give you their Wi-Fi password on the condition that you make a purchase.

Visitors travelling to the UK with EU tariffs are able to use their devices abroad without being affected by data roaming charges. Users will be charged the same rates for data, SMS services and voice calls as they would pay at home. This situation may change once the UK has left the EU.

Post

Standard post in the UK is handled by Royal Mail. There are Royal Mail post office branches located throughout London, which are generally open from 9am–5:30pm Mon–Fri and until 12:30pm Sat.

You can buy 1st-class, 2nd-class and international stamps in post offices, shops and supermarkets. Distinctive red post boxes are located on main streets throughout the city.

Taxes and Refunds

VAT (Value Added Tax) is charged at 20% and almost always included in the marked price. Stores offering tax-free shopping display a distinctive sign and (for non-EU residents) will provide you with a VAT 407 form to validate when you leave the country.

Discount Cards

London can be a very expensive city, but there a number of ways in which costs can be reduced, and many museums are free. Students and under-18s pay lower admission to many exhibitions, and holders of an ISIC (International Student Identity Card) or IYTC (International Youth Travel Card) are eligible for a range of other discounts. A number of visitor passes and discount cards are available online and from participating tourist offices. These cards are not free, so consider carefully how many of the offers you are likely to take advantage of before buying one. For a full list of the options available, consult the **Visit London** website. One such card is the **London Pass**, which offers free entry to more than 80 of the city's top attractions, fast-track entry to some busier sights, money-off selected tours and discounts in participating shops and restaurants, with the option of adding unlimited travel.

London Pass w londonpass.com
Visit London w visitlondon.com

INDEX

ACKNOWLEDGMENTS

Dorling Kindersley would like to extend special thanks to the following people for their contribution: Michelle Crane, Syed Mohammad Farhan, Rashika Kachroo, Shanker Prasad, Rohit Rojal.

The publisher would like to thank the following for their kind permission to reproduce their photographs:

Key: a-above; b-below/bottom; c-centre; f-far; l-left; r-right; t-top

123RF.com: Christian Mueller 86b.

4Corners: Maurizio Rellini 4-5b, 68b.

Alamy Stock Photo: Arcaid Images / Richard Bryant 89tl; Colin Bain 35t; Guy Bell 100t; Nigel Blacker 30tl; Ian Dagnall 79clb; Exflow 88bl; Malcolm Fairman 41t; Nicola Ferrari 58b; Garden Photo World / David C Phillips 62b; Alex Hare 99tr; Angelo Hornak 52crb; Ianni Dimitrov Pictures 18t; incamerastock 71cr; Jansos 74b; LH Images 91cla; London Picture Library 40b; Mark Phillips 42t; Photopat / Tate Modern, London / SUPERFLEX © DACS 2018 One Two Three Swing! 63cb; Enrico Della Pietra 28b; PjrWindows 34b; Laurence Prax 25bl; RayArt Graphics 22b; Robertharding / Adam Woolfitt 10clb; Roger

Cracknell 01 / classic 76bl; Peter Scholey 54br; Scott Hortop Travel 44bl; Adrian Seal 59tl; Ian Shaw 65tc; Homer Sykes 43br; Roger Tillberg 64crb; travelpix 79cr; Trevor Smithers ARPS 35crb; Gregory Wrona 16b.

AWL Images: Alex Robinson 90b; Mark Sykes 82tr; Travel Pix Collection 6b.

Depositphotos Inc: masterlu 50b.

Dreamstime.com: Anyaivanova 26bl; Anthony Baggett 37tl; Chris Dorney 7tl; Fuzja44 66-7b; Wei Huang 84-5bc; Imrandr 70cra; Juliengrondin 56tl; Madrabothair 32br, 60tr; Ac Manley 69tl; Minacarson 45tl; Dilyana Nikolova 80clb; Andrey Omelyanchuk 12br; Jozef Sedmak 21tl; Christopher Smith 78b; Tose 14-5b; Ufuk Uyanik 17t.

Getty Images: Dan Kitwood 45cla; Loop Images / Neil Tingle 92br; oversnap 94b; Peter Phipp 64br.

Historic Royal Palaces: Nick Guttridge 51clb.

iStockphoto.com: Alphotographic 63br; Leonid Andronov 11tl; anyaivanova 51t; Bombaert 46b; Dan Bridge 96tr; chameleonseye 72tr; Angelina Dimitrova 38t;

Elenathewise 19br; garyperkin 96b; ivanastar 2t; matthewleesdixon 15tl; MichaelUtech 23tl; Nikada 3tl; onebluelight 95t; RomanBabakin 17crb; sharrocks 83br; sjhaytov 70tl; stockinasia 29clb, 48-9tc; taikrixel 8bl; _ultraforma_ 98b; whitemay 13tc, ZambeziShark 18cr.

London Design Museum: Hufton + Crow 87crb.

National Portrait Gallery, London: 24t.

The Trustees of the Natural History Museum, London: 80b.

Robert Harding Picture Library: Eurasia 13cb; Markus Lange 81tl.

Image courtesy of the Saatchi Gallery, London: Steve White / Installation c̓ Champagne Life

exhibition 75tl.

courtesy Science M Group: © Plastiqı Photography 81

Courtesy of t̓ Sir John Soa̓ Caro Comm Gardner 36̓

ZSL Londo

For furth̓ www.dki̓